The Art of Brazilian Cooking

The Art of Brazilian Cooking

By Sandra Cuza
Photography by Mauro Holanda

PELICAN PUBLISHING COMPANY
GRETNA 2012

641.5981
C993

Library of Congress Cataloging-in-Publication Data

Cuza, Sandra.
 The art of Brazilian cooking / by Sandra Cuza ; photography by Mauro Holanda.
  p. cm.
 Includes index.
 ISBN 978-1-4556-1645-9 (hardcover : alk. paper) -- ISBN 978-1-4556-1646-6
(e-book) 1. Cooking, Brazilian. I. Title.
 TX716.B6C89 2012
 641.59'2698--dc23
                                    2012008174

Food styling by Tereza Galante

Printed in China
Published by Pelican Publishing Company, Inc.
1000 Burmaster Street, Gretna, Louisiana 70053

This book is for my husband, Luis. Without his skill and expertise with the computer, his encouragement, his willingness to sample every recipe, and his companionship at the feira *and in the kitchen, this book could not have been written and my sense of humor would have been lost.*

Contents

Acknowledgments

Special thanks go to Deborah Riveros for suggesting this book and contributing so many recipes and to Adeline Remy for her recipes and her research into the culinary history of Brazil, including the origin and background of the fruits grown here.

I am grateful to the many friends who have sampled the recipe tests and have given their honest evaluations and to those who have provided guidance over the years in mastering this cuisine and have contributed recipes that have been incorporated into my collection. I am indebted to those that have provided recipes specifically for this book, especially Dulce Muniz; Vanda Pereira de Souza; Lenina Pomeranz; Laura de Borba; Jean Boyd; Maria de Fatima Honorato; Chef Claudia Anailde; Jean Smith; Susie Lund; Chef Fernando Ricardo Couto and his wife, Christina, owners of Confraria do Sabor restaurant; Dona Teta; Dona Anita; and Marlice Bach. I also wish to thank Chef Quintin Geenen de Saint Maur and his publisher, A&A Communicação Ltda., for allowing me to include two recipes from his book *Muito Prazer, Brasil.*

Thanks also to my agent, Al Longden, for his unfailing help and support, and to my editors, Nina Kooij and Heather Green.

I feel extremely lucky to have been able to work with food photographer Mauro Holanda, whose enthusiasm for this project was equaled only by his enormous skill and creativity, and with food designer Tereza Galante, who deserves a special bow for her artistry in this field. Thanks also to the photographer's assistant, Jennifer Besse.

Both Tereza and I thank the following São Paulo establishments: Amoa Konoya Arte Indigena, M. Dragonetti, Roberto Simões Casa, Roupa de Mesa, and Stella Ferraz Cerámica.

Introduction

For decades, exotic Brazil has been the consummate ideal for beaches, dental floss bikinis, samba music, and beautiful women but very little else about the country ever drew the attention of the United States public. Only recently, when former president Lula led the country to a position of worldwide importance, both diplomatically and economically, was awareness and curiosity aroused. After the announcement that Brazil would host both the 2014 World Cup and 2016 Olympic Games, there was a surge of enthusiasm concerning all aspects of Brazil. Bossa nova and samba music were revived, and a rash of carnivals sprang up across America. Portuguese newspapers and on-line publications flourished while increasing numbers of universities and language schools offered opportunities for exchange students and courses in Portuguese.

Not surprisingly, cuisine generated the keenest interest. Although small Brazilian cafés had existed for many years in Brazilian- and Portuguese-immigrant enclaves, the arrival of the upscale restaurant Fogo de Chão in the United States ushered in a wave of high-quality Brazilian restaurants. Specialty shops began to carry Brazilian foodstuffs, and an enterprising butcher in Pennsylvania devoted one day a month to slaughtering a cow in order to provide the cuts of meat favored by Brazilians. Meanwhile, adventurous gourmet cooks searched for recipes. But what exactly is Brazilian cuisine?

Modern Brazilian fare is rooted in a combination of Portuguese and African cookery and, to a much lesser extent, that of the indigenous Indians. Portuguese explorer Pedro Alvares Cabral landed in Bahia in 1500, beginning the influx of Portuguese immigrants, followed by the first slave ship in 1538. Since slavery was not abolished until 1888 and 3.5 million Africans (six times the number brought to the U.S.) survived the Atlantic crossing, virtually every white Brazilian from Rio de Janeiro to Salvador owned at least one slave for the better part of three hundred years, and these slaves controlled the kitchens. Finding many familiar comestibles in their new environment—palm oil, coconut, bananas, nuts, peppers, and fish—African cooks used their traditional cooking methods, ingredients,

and techniques and combined them with the food of their masters, including *bacalhau,* or salt cod. Gradually indigenous foods and new cooking skills learned from the Indians were incorporated into their repertoire. Because relatively few Portuguese women had immigrated to Brazil, liaisons and occasional intermarriage between female slaves and masters was tolerated, and these unions firmly established the Portuguese/African diet. *Feijoada,* the national dish, which is religiously served for Wednesday and Saturday lunch throughout Brazil accompanied by ground, toasted manioc meal called *farofa,* comes directly from slave kitchens; the ultrasweet desserts made with eggs and sugar have their origins in Portugal.

When, in 1763, the capital of the colony moved from Salvador to Rio de Janeiro, the cuisine moved with it, remaining unchanged throughout the rule of Portuguese king João VI in the 1800s. Not until the arrival of the Japanese in 1908 as contract laborers on the São Paulo coffee plantations did the Brazilian diet—short on fruits, in a country where they were to be found in abundance, and vegetables in any form—alter radically. Within thirty years, thousands of Japanese had arrived, managed to purchase small farms, and were growing almost half of all fresh produce in the state, which they introduced to an urban São Paulo population that was just awakening to the delights of more sophisticated, less parochial cuisine. In the late nineteenth century and throughout the twentieth, Brazil welcomed Italian, Polish, and German immigrants to the south where they left an indelible mark on the food of that area.

Today, traditional fare still prevails in the smaller cities and rural areas of every state, particularly the Amazon, which is separated from the rest of the country by vast jungles and a network of rivers. Only local ingredients found in that region and nowhere else in Brazil are used in food preparation. Migrants to the city of São Paulo, however, brought their culinary arts with them. In this metropolis of 22 million people, distinctive regional culinary arts lost their edge, mixed and blended, and were transformed into the sophisticated dishes of São Paulo that have become known as Brazilian cuisine.

The Art of Brazilian Cooking introduces this cuisine, including traditional dishes, to the reader through São Paulo's *feiras,* the time-honored street markets that are an integral part of the country's culture. Both Brazilian feiras and the farmers' markets of America are held outdoors and sell from stalls. However, in São Paulo, the sellers are no longer farmers who bring their crops to the marketplace but are professional vendors who have specialized in one type of foodstuff, are licensed by the city, and work in a different feira every day of the week but Monday. These are not random moves; sellers are assigned specific locations in each of the markets and may not move from one designated spot to another or change feiras without the city's permission, although they may sell their stall, if they wish. Highly organized, present-day feiras are a continuum of pre-supermarket days when the city was smaller and the farmers were also the sellers, offering produce that was only available in the open-air market. Despite the crush and noise of an enormous city, the flavor of old-time markets has been preserved in the feiras of São Paulo.

Feiras vary considerably in size, variety of produce offered, and price. The street market featured in this book is fairly small—two blocks long— but many others are much larger, and at least two take place in football stadiums. The economic level of each neighborhood, rather than the size of the feira, determines both the foodstuffs sold and the prices asked. In the upscale Jardims district, for example, it is not difficult to find asparagus, baby lettuce, romaine, endive, French green beans, out-of-season strawberries, and imported cherries at the feira, all commanding high prices. Conversely, foodstuffs in a poor area would be restricted to carrots, cabbage, papaya, and other low-cost comestibles. The focus of *The Art of Brazilian Cooking* is a feira located in a mixed, downtown area that is the center of São Paulo's experimental theaters and, therefore, caters to a wide variety of tastes and pocketbooks. Although an extensive selection of food is offered at fair prices, exotic imported fruits and vegetables are missing.

In the state of São Paulo, the breadbasket of the country, huge trucks from the interior haul produce, dairy products, and poultry to either CEAGESP, the enormous wholesale market in the city of São Paulo, where ten thousand tons of food plus flowers are sold daily, or to a similarly large market located in nearby Serra do Cantereira. Fish are trucked from the coast around 3:00 A.M., and feira vendors converge on these markets to buy fresh food to sell that day. By 5:30 A.M., these vendors have left the wholesale markets and are setting up their stalls all over the city, arranging pieces of fruit and vegetables, mountains of eggs, and rows of fish in attractive, artistic displays. Customers, almost always residents of the surrounding area, begin to arrive at 7:00 A.M., dragging the wire, wheeled shopping carts that will soon be stuffed and overflowing. A little later, young boys appear, offering their services as *carregadores*, or porters, to carry purchases or pull the increasingly heavy carts, accompanying their temporary employer through the feira and then on to the patron's home.

From poor families, these boys will earn one or two reais (between $0.60 and $1.20 U.S.) per customer.

By 10:00 A.M., the feira is packed with buyers and noisy with the competing shouts of vendors as they broadcast their prices and wares. Oddly, although the feiras teem with strangers, they are some of the safest places in the city; in crime-prone São Paulo, theft in the street markets rarely happens. As early afternoon approaches, vendors' cries become more desperate, prices drop, and the bargain hunters move in along with street dwellers who wait to collect any discarded, unsold food. At 2:00 P.M., closing time is mandated so that city workers may clean up the premises before rush hour. Although there are exceptions, most of these street markets are two to three blocks long and held in city thoroughfares that are closed to traffic on feira days. Regardless of the weather, stalls are set up on both sides of the street in an arrangement that obstructs both traffic and the driveways of homes and businesses. Since feiras are a traditional part of the Brazilian culture, those affected take it in stride, uncomplainingly using alternative transportation routes and methods.

Who shops at the feira? Just about everyone. The arrival of supermarkets did not diminish the popularity of these markets, where the best prices and freshest foods were and are to be found, along with the expertise of vendors to advise and help in the selection of any product they sell. In past times, patrons depended on the feira not just for food but for socialization; this was where friends met, gossiped, and exchanged news before finally making purchases, always from the same vendors.

Prior to the 1970s, women in the upper and relatively small middle classes did not cook; this domestic chore was entrusted to hired help who shopped for the food they would then prepare in small, dark, badly equipped kitchens that were, no doubt, holdovers from slave days. Around the mid-1970s, the situation changed when a very upscale company that designed and sold efficient and beautiful kitchens arrived in São Paulo, and it became fashionable to include this room in the overall design of the home or apartment. Her interest piqued by a spacious and well-planned kitchen that was often the envy of her friends, the *dona da casa*, or lady of the house, gradually involved herself in the preparation of family and guest meals.

Today, feira shoppers are Brazilians of all classes who do not depend on the street market for social life and conversation but prefer the fresher foodstuffs of the feira to those of the supermarkets. Most feiras have a number of stalls selling the same type of produce, but shoppers invariably patronize the same vendors week after week because they like the selection of food carried by their chosen vendor and are confident that he or she will never cheat them on either price or quality. And although many of these male and female feira workers have little formal education, they invariably remember the likes and dislikes of their regular customers in each feira of the week, easily recall what every patron purchased last week, and counsel on items that are particularly outstanding or not really up to par.

Written by an American woman who has lived since the 1990s in São Paulo preparing the food of the country, *The Art of Brazilian Cooking* is a guide for those who want to recreate Brazilian cuisine in their own kitchens with ease and confidence. Throughout the book, authentic Brazilian recipes using ingredients available in the United States are offered, together with interesting histories and folk beliefs connected to the various foodstuffs.

The Art of Brazilian Cooking

1

Onions, Garlic, Rice, and Beans

At 7:00 A.M. my husband and I begin our tour of the feira, starting with the stand that sells the basic Brazilian diet, the food that has kept the poor alive for centuries and is now a part of Brazilian culture. Today, it is difficult to find any Brazilian meal that doesn't include these four staples, the first two in almost any cooked main or side dish, and rice and/or beans as accompaniment to shrimp, chicken, meat, in a *feijoada*—the national dish—or as a simple supper. Traditionally, only white rice is served in homes and restaurants, but recently whole-grain rice has begun to appear on the tables of more experimental cooks; at this stand, we can find all types and grades of rice along with cornmeal and many varieties of dried beans. By and large, the same beans are found in both the U.S. and Brazil, with the exception of limas, which are unavailable here, and *cordas,* which I think are unobtainable in the States.

Vendors offer heads of garlic arranged in an attractive design and onions sorted according to origin, size, and type at one end of the stand; at the other end, cornmeal and beans are displayed. These dry foodstuffs are bought in

bulk by the stand owners who package them in half-kilo (1.1 pounds) plastic bags for resale to the public. As is the case with all the stands, a clothesline is run from one support to the other and is positioned just above eye level. Prices are marked on pieces of paper and clipped, with clothespins, to the line above each section of food, an arrangement that allows the vendor to quickly mark down prices throughout the day.

As is our custom, we stop first at the stand owned by Armando and his wife, Keiko, both of whom have worked in feiras since the 1980s. Keiko now works just at this Sunday feira while Armando's only day off is Monday, when all feiras are closed. In accordance with customary good manners in Brazil, before doing business we always exchange greetings with the seller, comment on the good or bad weather, and inquire about the vendor's health and family. As Armando artfully arranges a pyramid of garlic heads and the couple's adult daughter sorts onions, we ask Keiko if their two grown children who are living in Japan will be visiting soon. When she sadly replies that the distance and cost of airfare severely limit any visits, I can truly sympathize since we are similarly curbed in our travels to the U.S. Looking around, I realize that their third son, a computer-science student at a local college who usually helps out on Sunday, is missing and Keiko explains that he is studying for an exam. She thanks us for the chocolate-chip cookies we brought last weekend, and I remember some of the gifts she has given us over the years, including a black-lacquered Japanese tray and small Buddha.

Pleasantries over, I get down to serious business and bend over the red onions and garlic.

Onions, Garlic, Rice, and Beans

Baião de Dois
Dance of Two

This is one of those basic rice and bean dishes found everywhere and is often served with fish or chicken. I have found that, with the cheese, it is perfect for lunch or a light supper accompanied only by a salad and crusty bread. In Brazil, it's made with *corda* beans—brown black-eyed peas—but I have successfully substituted pintos. Here, jack cheese has replaced *coalho*, but any mild, white cheese may be used.

    2 cups pinto beans, soaked overnight
    2 cups rice
    4 tbsp. butter
    1 hot red pepper, minced
    1 green pepper, chopped
    1 large onion, chopped
    4 cloves garlic, minced
    ⅓ lb. jack cheese
    Chopped parsley
    Chopped cilantro

Cook the beans and rice separately, reserving the cooking liquid from the beans. While they are cooking, melt the butter in a large skillet and sauté the hot red pepper, green pepper, onion, and garlic. Grate a half-cup of the cheese and cut the remainder in thin slices. Add the rice, beans, 1 cup of bean liquid, and the cheese to the frying pan, heat the mixture, and turn into a serving bowl, sprinkling with the parsley and cilantro.

Serves 8.

Feijão Preto com Bananas
Black Beans with Bananas

This is the perfect accompaniment to almost any simple chicken, fish, or meat dish. The beans may be prepared ahead of time and reheated while the bananas sauté. Although the recipe calls for plantains, those starchy bananas that retain their shape when cooked, I have successfully used ordinary bananas in this dish when plantains were not available. In such an event, sauté the bananas very lightly and fold them carefully into the beans to avoid dissolving the fruit.

1 cup dry black beans
1-2 tbsp. olive oil
¾ cup onion, finely chopped
2 cloves garlic, minced
¾ cup red bell pepper, finely chopped
½ tsp. dry oregano
½ tsp. dry cumin
1 bay leaf
Salt and pepper to taste
2-3 plantains cut in thick slices
1 tsp. wine vinegar

Rinse the beans and soak overnight. Transfer the beans and soaking liquid to a pot and set aside. In a separate pan, heat a minimum of olive oil and sauté the onion, garlic, bell pepper, oregano, and cumin until tender. Add to the beans along with the bay leaf and additional water, if needed. Cover and cook for 1 hour or until done, adding water from time to time if necessary. When the beans are done, salt and pepper to taste. Just before serving, sauté the plantains and add to the bean mixture along with the wine vinegar.

Serves 4.

Caldinho do Feijão
Dulce's Bean Soup

On a winter night when the temperature dropped to 8 degrees, this steaming soup was served in small ceramic cups along with wine and glasses of *cachaça* at an event in one of the experimental theaters. Soup, either hot or cold, is frequently served in demitasse cups, without spoons or saucers, at large luncheons, but this was the first time I had experienced soup at an opening. It was absolutely delicious, and when asked for the recipe, Dulce Muniz, actress and director of the Teatro Studio 184 and also creator of the soup, was delighted to oblige.

Traditionally, the problem with Brazilian recipes has been the fact that they are very vague; sometimes no oven temperatures are given, no pan sizes are indicated even for cakes, cooking time is not designated, and there may be no clear idea of how many people the recipe will serve. In this instance, the ingredients had been listed along with only a rough idea of amounts and

it took a few tests before I was able to duplicate the flavor of her creation. The soup should have a bite but not be terribly spicy. If fresh red chili pepper isn't available, any fresh or canned pepper may be substituted.

    4 cups cooked beans (pinto or red; no white or black)
    4 cups water (more or less)
    2 tbsp. olive oil
    2 medium onions, chopped
    1 tbsp. minced ginger
    1 cup loosely packed fresh cilantro leaves
    1 fresh red pepper without seeds
    ¼ lb. bacon, cooked very crisp
    1 tbsp. olive oil
    2 cloves garlic, minced
    Salt and pepper to taste

Pulse the cooked beans in a blender, gradually adding water until the soup is almost smooth and slightly thinner than you want the finished product to be. In a pan, sauté the onions in 2 tbsp. olive oil until wilted. Add the cooked onions, ginger, cilantro, and red pepper to the soup, blend, and return to the cooking pot. Crumble the bacon and add it to the soup. Set aside. Add 1 tbsp. olive oil to the pan in which the onions were sautéed and sauté the garlic, cooking only until it is a very light tan, as it will turn bitter with browning. Add to the soup, salt and pepper to taste, and cook over low heat for 20 minutes or until it has amalgamated and thickened, stirring from time to time. Add salt and pepper and remove from the fire.

To serve, Brazilians use a black ceramic pot with a lid but any attractive soup pot will do. Accompany it with the following, each in a small dish to be passed around the table.

    1. 4-6 large cloves garlic, sautéed
    2. Fresh ginger
    3. Cilantro leaves, finely chopped
    4. 6 fresh red peppers without seeds, minced

Serves 6.

Caldo Toscano
Tuscan Soup

Ribollita is an Italian vegetable soup from Tuscany that may contain any combination of vegetables, but it always includes dried white beans and bread. This delicious version speaks to the Italian immigrants who brought the recipe with them and, as Brazilians, then abbreviated it.

1 cup dried white beans
½ cup chopped onion
1 medium leek, white part only, finely chopped
3 cloves garlic, minced
2 tbsp. olive oil
¾ lb. cabbage, both red and white
4 cups vegetable stock (homemade or bouillon cube)
1 tsp. fresh thyme
Salt and pepper
4 slices of Italian bread, toasted

Wash the beans, drain, and soak overnight in water, covering by at least 2 inches. In the morning, cook until done (the length of time depends on the age of the beans, but it will be anywhere from 1 to 2 hours). Meanwhile, sauté the onion, leek, and garlic in oil. Drain the cooked beans and combine with the onion mixture, cabbage, stock, and seasonings. Cook until the cabbage is done, adding

more stock, if necessary, and adjusting the seasonings. Put one slice of toast in the bottom of each soup plate, then pour the soup over the toast. Accompany with more toasted Italian bread. Serve immediately to preserve the beautiful purple and white color contrast. After a few hours, the dish will be completely lavender.

Serves 4.

Feijão de Tutu
Bean Tutu

This recipe originated in the neighboring state of Minas Gerais and is one of those recipes with endless variations. Traditionally, it is served with thinly sliced, cooked kale and rice and can also be garnished with chopped, hard-cooked eggs and scallions. Sometimes the beans are mashed, and it often accompanies grilled meat.

3 cups cooked black beans with liquid
Manioc meal or cornmeal, enough to thicken beans
2 tbsp. vinegar
¼ cup bacon, cut in pieces
½ lb. pork sausage, sliced
1 bay leaf
2 cloves garlic, minced
1 onion, thinly sliced
Kale, if desired

Heat beans, mash in their liquid, and add enough manioc or cornmeal to make a mush. Add the vinegar and reserve. In another pan, fry the bacon and sausage and add the bay leaf then the garlic. Mix in the beans and stir well to blend. Fry the onion slices and, if using, separately sauté the kale. Mound the beans on a platter and cover with onion slices. Surround beans with cooked kale, if it is used.

Serves 4.

Feijão Tropeiro
Cattle Driver's Beans

This is a dish originating in the south of Brazil, where cowboys tend herds of cattle and where the cuisine relies heavily on pork and beef.

2 cups uncooked kidney beans, soaked overnight
2 tbsp. corn oil

2 oz. pork rinds, cut in pieces
4 oz. smoked bacon
5 oz. pork loin, roasted and cut in pieces
1½ tbsp. minced garlic
2 large eggs
2 big leaves of kale, sliced very finely
1 medium onion, diced
1 cup manioc flour or cornmeal
¼ cup parsley, minced
¼ cup cilantro, minced
Salt, pepper, and hot pepper, to taste

Cook the beans without seasonings and set aside. Fry the pork rinds in oil and add the bacon and roasted pork loin. When cooked, add ½ tbsp. of minced garlic. Make a space in the middle of the meat and scramble the eggs, adding more minced garlic to the eggs. Add the kale, the onion, and 1 tbsp. of garlic. Mix. Still cooking, add the beans slowly then add the manioc flour or cornmeal, parsley, cilantro, salt, pepper, and hot pepper. Gently mix. Serve with rice and a salad.

Serves 6.

Arroz Integral Temperado
Seasoned Brown Rice

This is a more modern and sophisticated recipe, reflecting both the contemporary Brazilian interest in health and a traditional tendency to combine unlikely ingredients.

1 cup brown rice
2 cups water
1 medium carrot, cubed
½ cup green beans, chopped
1 onion, chopped
2 tbsp. oil or butter
½ cup cashew nuts, chopped
½ cup dark grapes, halved
Green onions and parsley, chopped
1 cup corn, cooked
Salt to taste
2 tbsp. toasted sesame seeds

Cook the rice and set aside. Over a pot of boiling water, steam the carrot and green beans. In a separate pan, sauté the onion in oil or butter. Combine all of the ingredients except the sesame seeds, mix well, and add salt to taste. Sprinkle with sesame seeds.

Serves 4.

Risoto de Rúcula, Tomate Seco e Mussarela
Arugula, Dried Tomato, and Mozzarella Risotto

Risottos are very popular in Brazil, due to the large number of Italian immigrants, and are made with a wide variety of ingredients, ranging from

squash to salt cod to dried beef. Arugula was never added to cooked dishes until Hamilton Mello Junior, chef in São Paulo's I Vitelloni Pizzeria, included it as one of his toppings. Now it is a common part of the city's cuisine.

7 oz. dried tomatoes in oil
2 tbsp. olive oil
½ small onion, chopped
4 oz. arugula, shredded
¾ cup *arborio* rice
½ cup white wine
1½ qt. beef or chicken stock (approximately)
7 oz. fresh mozzarella, cubed
2 tbsp. butter
⅓ cup grated Parmesan

Drain the tomatoes thoroughly; chop and sauté the tomatoes with the onion and half the arugula in olive oil. Add rice and stir for a few moments, coating thoroughly with oil. Add the wine and allow to evaporate. Bring the stock to a simmer and gradually add to the rice, a ½ cup at a time, while stirring. Only when the rice has absorbed the stock should more stock be added. It will take 20 to 30 minutes to cook the rice to al dente; do not cook to a mush. When done, remove from the fire, immediately add the remainder of the arugula and the mozzarella, and stir well. Add the butter and Parmesan, mix thoroughly, and serve.

Serves 6-7.

Onions, Garlic, Rice, and Beans

Risoto de Arroz Vermelho com Carne de Porco
Risotto with Red Rice and Pork

Although white rice has been a staple in Brazil for centuries, brown, black, and red rice are relative newcomers to the country. Considered exotic, red and black rice can be found only in upscale markets and appear only on the menus of the better restaurants. This recipe is an interesting twist on the usual risotto. If homemade beef stock is not available, canned stock, diluted consommé, or a beef cube can be used.

½ lb. pork, cut in small cubes
2 cups dry white wine
2 sprigs rosemary
1 stalk basil
1 tbsp. margarine
1 onion, chopped
½ cup *arborio* rice
1 cup white wine
2 cups or more beef stock, preferably homemade
Salt and pepper, to taste
1 cup red rice, cooked as brown rice
½ cup or more freshly grated parmesan

Combine the pork with dry white wine, rosemary, and basil and marinate for 1 hour. Drain the meat, sauté in margarine in a large pot until brown. Add the onion and cook until transparent. Add the *arborio* rice and cook for a few moments, stirring constantly to coat the grains with margarine. Add the 1 cup of white wine and cook on medium-low heat until it evaporates. Meanwhile, bring the stock to a boil and add ½ cup stock to the rice mixture. When the stock is almost absorbed, add another ½ cup and continue this process until the rice is soft and al dente, not mushy. Stir almost constantly so that the rice doesn't stew in the liquid and become soggy. When the rice is done, combine with salt and pepper, red rice, and cheese. Mix and serve immediately with additional cheese to pass at the table.

Serves 6-8.

Arroz Biro-Biro
Rice Biro-Biro

This dish was first presented in an elegant São Paulo restaurant where Biro-Biro, a famous and well-liked football player, happened to be dining. Since the dish resembled the appearance of the sportsman's hair, it became known as Rice Biro-Biro. It is the perfect accompaniment to any simple main dish including grilled fish, fried or roasted chicken, lamb chops, or barbequed meat. Everyone loves it and any leftovers work well the next day as fried rice.

1½ cups uncooked rice
½ small onion, chopped
3 scallions, with tops, sliced
2 tbsp. margarine
2 slices bacon, fried and crumbled
¼ cup parsley, chopped
2 eggs, fried with barely cooked yolks
1 large potato, julienned and sautéed

Onions, Garlic, Rice, and Beans

Cook the rice according to directions for cooking white rice *(arroz branco)* covered in this chapter. Set aside. Sauté the onion and scallions in margarine. Add the rice, bacon, and parsley. Cut the eggs in pieces and add to rice along with the potatoes. Salt to taste. Mix and serve.

Serves 4.

Arroz com Lula
Rice with Squid

This is a quickly prepared Brazilian way to present rice as a principal dish. Be sure to monitor the rice as it cooks; the amount of water required in this recipe depends on both the squid and the rice, and more water may be needed to prevent scorching.

1 lb. small squid, cleaned and cut into rings
1 tbsp. garlic, minced
3 tbsp. oil
1 large onion, finely chopped
5 cloves garlic, minced
2 cups raw white rice, well washed
½ cup dry white wine
Salt and pepper, to taste
A few threads of saffron, ground between the fingers
1½ cups or more boiling water
2 tbsp. butter
¼ cup scallions, washed and sliced

Wash the squid well and season with 1 tbsp. garlic. Set aside. In a wide pan, heat the oil and sauté the onion and 5 cloves garlic until transparent. Add the squid and sauté briefly, then pour in the rice and cook for 5 minutes, stirring. Add the white wine, salt, pepper, and saffron and mix well. Cover with boiling water, replace the lid, and cook on low heat for 15 to 20 minutes or until the rice is tender. Check from time to time and if the mixture is dry, add a bit of boiling water.

When the rice is ready, turn off the fire, add the butter and scallions, and mix well. Replace the lid and allow to rest for 10 minutes before serving.

Serves 5-6.

Arroz Branco
White Rice

Providing plain white rice as an accompaniment to other dishes is often mandatory when preparing Brazilian cuisine. This method of cooking is always successful.

¾ cup rice
1 tbsp. vegetable oil
2 cloves garlic, minced
1 cup water
Juice of ¼ lemon

Wash the rice in a sieve and drain well. Heat the oil in a saucepan, add the garlic, and sauté until lightly brown. Add the water, bring to a boil, and squeeze the lemon juice into the water. Add the rice, cover the pan, and bring to a boil. Immediately lower the heat and cook over a very low fire for 20 minutes. Fluff the rice and serve.

Serves 2-3.

Frango com Molho de Cebola
Chicken with Onion Sauce

Some years ago, packaged soups were introduced to Brazil and were enthusiastically received, although they were not always used as the basis for soup. A working mother with two pre-teenage boys, Laura de Borba has developed this easily prepared, delicious dish, which she serves to her family after a busy workday as well as to guests on festive occasions. No browning is necessary, as the chicken becomes golden brown during the baking process.

5 chicken quarters (thigh and drumstick), skin on or skinless as you prefer
½ cup dry packaged onion soup
2½ cups malt beer

Arrange the chicken quarters in a baking pan and sprinkle all sides with the onion soup; marinate for 1 hour. Pour the malt beer over the chicken and bake at 325 degrees F until done—about 45 minutes. Turn once and check to see that there is sufficient liquid. If necessary, add a little water as this will become the sauce. Serve with rice or mashed potatoes and the sauce.

Serves 5.

2

Seafood

Because the country boasts three thousand miles of coastland and a vast network of rivers in the interior, fish and other seafood have always played a prominent role in the Brazilian diet. Feiras generally offer only the fish, crustaceans, and mollusks locally available, which means that, with the exception of salmon and tuna, São Paulo ferias have little imported fish or seafood from northern Brazil.

We stop for fish at a stand owned by an Asian family who are also proprietors of a large seafood company that delivers to restaurants and individuals. Although various members of the family are always present, Marta, our fishmonger, is the star and an enormously popular one. Forty-seven years old, but looking much younger, Marta has worked all her adult life in the feira and, for the

past twenty-three years, has been employed by this company. Lively and with a quick sense of humor, she can be depended upon to tell her customers which fish are fresh, which to avoid, and whether or not the price is right.

The seafood, which arrives in a large refrigerated truck parked just behind the stand, is beautifully displayed on beds of ice, beginning with the various sizes of shrimp, clams, and calamari at one end of the counter and progressing to shiny, whole fish arranged according to type. Although some of the more popular, less expensive fish have been filleted or cut into steaks upon arrival early in the morning, there are no precut, packaged fish. Like all feira fishmongers, the owners and employees usually debone, slice, fillet, and leave the head and tail on or take them off of fish; shell the shrimp; clean the calamari; or whatever else the customer might want, all free of charge and done to order. In addition, Marta knows the preferred method of cooking any fish she sells and can recommend ways of preparing them. This is no minor accomplishment since Brazilian waters have a dizzying number of these vertebrates, all of them unfamiliar to North Americans. In these recipes, use firm, white-fleshed fish with mild flavor unless otherwise specified.

Peixe com Banana e Geléia de Pimenta
Fish with Banana and Hot Pepper Jelly

Always served with rice, this dish is easily doubled for a dinner party and is liked by everyone, even those who do not normally care for spicy food.

2 lb. sea bass or other mild, firm fish fillets, skin on
2 tbsp. olive oil
2 tsp. grated fresh ginger
⅓ cup flour
1 tsp. crushed herbs (thyme and marjoram, if possible)
1½ tbsp. butter, melted
3 bananas, sliced diagonally
2 tbsp. hot pepper jelly
⅓ cup sliced almonds, toasted

Rub fillets with olive oil, sprinkle with ginger on the side without skin, and marinate for 15 minutes. Combine flour and herbs, and dust fillets with mixture. Broil for approximately 10 minutes on each side or sauté until done. Meanwhile, melt the butter in another frying pan and sauté the bananas until warm (about 3-4 minutes), being careful not to mash them. In a separate pan, warm the pepper jelly. Arrange the fish on a platter and pour pepper jelly over the fish. Sprinkle the fish with toasted almonds and serve with bananas on one side.

Serves 4.

Peixe com Papaia e Banana
Fish with Papaya and Banana

This is an easy dish, another good one to serve guests, and it looks spectacular.

4-5 oz. fish fillets
Salt and pepper, to taste
3 ripe, firm bananas or, preferably, plantains
¼ cup fresh lemon or lime juice
1 papaya, peeled and seeded
¼ cup butter, melted
¼ cup butter, browned
⅓ cup chopped parsley

Arrange fillets in single layer in a buttered baking pan. Sprinkle with salt and pepper. Peel bananas and slice lengthwise, then dip in lime juice. Slice papaya lengthwise in ½-inch slices. Arrange fruit slices alongside fish and drizzle ¼ cup butter over all. Bake at 400 degrees F for 8-10 minutes. Meanwhile, brown the rest of the butter and add parsley and 2 tbsp. of remaining lime juice. Pour over cooked fish and fruits and serve.

Serves 4.

Peixe com Banana e Uvas
Fish with Banana and Grapes

Use either the small, seedless black grapes or the larger variety in this simple recipe, which is delicious and visually dramatic. If you use grapes with seeds, halve and seed them before adding to the sauce.

4 top-quality fish fillets
1 tbsp. oil
4 plantains
2 tbsp. butter
Pepper, to taste
6 tbsp. butter
1 onion, chopped
2 cloves garlic, minced
Salt to taste
1 tbsp. vegetable oil
1 cup black grapes
Juice of 1 lemon
1 tbsp. minced cilantro
Arugula

Sauté the fillets in 1 tbsp. oil. Cut the plantains in half lengthwise and, in another skillet, sauté them in 2 tbsp. butter. Pepper to taste. Meanwhile, melt the 6 tbsp. butter in a saucepan and, when it turns light brown, add the onion and garlic. Cook until the onion is transparent and add salt, 1 tbsp. vegetable oil, grapes, lemon juice, and cilantro. Continue to cook for a minute or two or until the mixture is hot. To serve, arrange the plantains in the center of a platter, top with fish, and pour the grape sauce over. Surround with arugula.

Serves 4.

Salmão Assado com Açúcar Mascavel
Baked Salmon with Brown Sugar

Salmon, one of the few imported fish, is very popular in Brazil and can be found in most of the feiras. This is salmon with a tropical twist.

1½ tbsp. butter, melted
Juice of ½ lime
½ large orange, juice and zest
Salt and pepper, to taste
4-5 oz. salmon fillets
2 tbsp. brown sugar
1 tsp. red pepper flakes
1 large clove garlic, minced

Preheat the oven to 425 degrees F. Line a shallow baking dish, large enough to hold the salmon without overlapping, with aluminum foil and grease with a little of the melted butter. Combine the lime and orange juice with salt and pepper and pour into the baking pan. Add the salmon, turning to coat with the marinade. Let marinate at room temperature for 20 minutes, turning the fillets once.

In a small dish, combine the orange zest, brown sugar, red pepper flakes, and minced garlic. Rub the marinated salmon with the brown sugar mixture and drizzle with the remaining melted butter. Bake for 8-12 minutes or until done.

Serves 4.

Pescada com Quinua
Fish with Quinoa

The various components of this dish may be assembled at your leisure before the meal is to be served, with only the fish cooked at the last moment.

½ cup quinoa
1½ cups water
3 tbsp. chopped red onion
2 cloves garlic, minced

2 tbsp. olive oil
½ small red bell pepper, finely chopped
½ small zucchini, finely chopped
½ small carrot, finely chopped
2 scallions, thinly sliced (use some of the green tops)
2 tbsp. white wine vinegar
Salt and pepper, to taste
2 cod fillets or similar fish

Relish
1 tbsp. grated ginger
3 tbsp. chopped red onion
3 small chilies, minced, or to taste
1 tbsp. chopped nuts (cashew or Brazil)
2 tbsp. chopped apple
2 tbsp. chopped pear
1 tbsp. lime juice
1 tbsp. each chopped cilantro, dill, and mint
Salt, to taste
Olive oil

Combine the quinoa and water, cover, and simmer for 13 minutes. Drain. Meanwhile, sauté the red onion and garlic in oil, then combine with quinoa, red pepper, zucchini, and carrot, all cut to the same size. Add the scallions and vinegar, taste for salt and pepper, and set aside at room temperature.

Mix all relish ingredients together and reserve at room temperature.

Sauté the fish on both sides in olive oil. Serve the fish with the quinoa mixture on one side and the relish on the other.

Serves 2.

Moqueca
Brazilian Fish Stew

A *moqueca* is a seafood stew and can include any combination of shrimp, fish, squid, clams, scallops, and lobster or just fish. This basic recipe can be varied according to your taste and ingredients on hand. Add and subtract as you like—a splash of *cachaça,* less tomatoes, a green bell pepper, more garlic— it will still be Brazilian and authentic.

1 large onion, sliced
3 tbsp. olive oil
1 tbsp. *dendê* oil (optional)
3 large cloves garlic, minced
2 bell peppers, any color, sliced
1 or more chili peppers, minced
4 medium tomatoes, peeled and sliced
Salt, to taste
1½ cups coconut milk
2 lb. seafood
Fresh cilantro, chopped

Sauté the onion in olive oil and, if it is used, *dendê* oil for a few minutes. Add the garlic, bell peppers, chili peppers, and tomatoes and sauté for a few minutes. Adjust the salt, add the coconut milk, and cook over low heat for about 8 minutes or until the bell peppers are soft. Top with the seafood, cover, and cook until the seafood is done. Serve sprinkled with chopped cilantro.

Serves 6.

Linguado com Sálvia e Purê de Couve-flor
Sole with Sage and Purée of Cauliflower

Cauliflower plays a major role in this recipe, but, interestingly enough, when puréed, the delicate flavor is unidentifiable as cauliflower. Sole, a first cousin to *linguado*, is enhanced by the sage butter and pairs beautifully with the purée.

1 medium cauliflower
2 basil leaves
1 tbsp. lemon juice
1 tbsp. vegetable oil
½ cup butter, clarified (instructions below)
10 sage leaves or more, as you like
1½ lb. sole fillets
2 tbsp. butter

Break the cauliflower into florets and wash well. In a large saucepan, combine the cauliflower, basil, and lemon juice, add water to cover, and cook until soft. Immediately process in the blender, starting at the lowest speed, until puréed and then return to the pan along with the 1 tbsp. vegetable oil. If there is excess liquid, evaporate it over medium heat.

Over low heat, melt ½ cup butter. Remove the milky substance that forms on the bottom and the foam on top and fry the sage leaves until crunchy. Remove from the heat.

Season the fish with salt and pepper and sauté it in a hot skillet in 2 tbsp. butter. Reheat the cauliflower purée. Arrange the fillets on one side of a platter with the cauliflower purée alongside and bathe the fish with warm sage butter.

Serves 4.

Filé Baiana
Baiana Fillet

This is another recipe that was passed to us verbally by a Brazilian friend while she prepared and cooked the fish for an informal dinner. The dish was nameless, she explained, until her cousin suggested that the recipe probably originated in Bahia; from then on, it was called Baiana Fish.

4 large, thick fillets, skin on
Salt and pepper
4 tbsp. Brazilian Spice (see index)
4 tbsp. olive oil
4-8 large cloves garlic, minced

Wash the fillets thoroughly and pat dry. Rub a little salt and pepper into the fish, followed by the Brazilian Spice. The amount depends on your personal preference and also the amount of pepper in the mix, but 1 tbsp. or less per large fillet should be ample. While rubbing the spices into the fish, beware of any stray or hidden bones.

Sauté the garlic in olive oil over low heat until it is light brown and spoon it onto the fillets. Drizzle the remaining oil over the fish and rub it in using a metal spoon. You need only enough to moisten the spices (1-1 ½ tbsp. per fillet).

Put the fish in a large, oiled baking pan, skin side down and bake at

350 degrees F for about 15-17 minutes or until it is almost done. At this point, the bottom three-quarters will be white and the top part still a bit pink. Move the pan close to the broiler and broil for another 5 minutes; remember that the fish will continue to cook after removing from the oven, so do not overcook. And do not flip the fish; if you don't have a broiler, finish cooking it in the oven.

Serves 4 hungry people.

Robalo com Capim-Santo e Vatapá
Fish with Lemongrass and *Vatapá*

In this dish, both *vatapá*, a classic Afro-Brazilian purée using either fresh or dried shrimp, and the fish crust have been flavored with lemongrass, an herb brought to Brazil by the Japanese. Although the list of ingredients is long, everything is reasonably easy to obtain, and the components of the dish may be made ahead of time and finished just before serving.

Seafood

Fish

4-5 oz. firm, white fish fillets
Juice of 1 lemon
Salt and pepper, to taste

Lemongrass Crust

2 tsp. minced onion
2 tsp. minced garlic
1 tbsp. oil
4 tbsp. breadcrumbs
4 tbsp. finely chopped parsley
1 tsp. finely chopped hot pepper
1 tbsp. finely chopped lemongrass stems
Salt and pepper, to taste

Vatapá

2 thick slices Italian bread
About ½ cup milk
2 tbsp. minced garlic
2 tbsp. minced onion
2 tbsp. olive oil
Salt and pepper, to taste
7 oz. small shrimp
2 tbsp. minced red bell pepper
2 tbsp. minced yellow bell pepper
1 tomato, cut in small cubes
2 tsp. finely chopped lemongrass stems
2 tsp. finely chopped ginger
1 tsp. minced hot pepper
⅔ cup unsweetened coconut milk
2 tbsp. chopped Brazil nuts
2 tbsp. chopped peanuts
1 tsp. _dendê_ oil (optional)
2 tbsp. minced parsley

Fish

Season the fish with lemon juice, salt, and pepper and reserve in the refrigerator.

Lemongrass Crust

Sauté the onion and garlic in oil, remove from the heat, and add the remaining ingredients.

Vatapá

Shred the slices of bread in the blender, turn into a small bowl, and add enough milk to moisten. Briefly sauté the garlic and onion in oil, season the shrimp with salt and pepper, and add to the skillet. When the shrimp has lost its transparency, add the bell peppers, tomato, lemongrass stems, ginger, and hot pepper. Sauté for 1-2 minutes and add the coconut milk, Brazil nuts, peanuts, *dende* oil (if used), and the bread from which any excess milk has been squeezed. Cook for 2 minutes, and beat in the blender to obtain a rough purée. Return to the skillet and, when ready to serve, adjust the salt and pepper, and cook for 1 minute.

To Serve

Bake the fillets in a hot oven (400 degrees F) for 5 minutes. Remove from the oven and cover each filet with the crust; return to the oven for 5-10 more minutes, depending on the thickness of the fillets. Reheat the *vatapá*, divide it among 4 plates, and top the purée with fish. Sprinkle with parsley.

Serves 4.

Peixe ao Molho Caiçara
Fish with *Caiçara* Sauce

This recipe was provided by Vanda Pereira de Souza who created the Orange and Yogurt Cake in the dessert section.

6 thin fish fillets (St. Peters, tilapia, sole, etc.)
3 cloves garlic, minced
½ cup white wine
Salt and pepper

Sauce

½ cup white wine
1 large onion, chopped
3 cloves garlic, minced
1 small hot pepper, minced
3 medium-size red bell peppers, roasted and peeled
1 tbsp. sugar
1½ cups natural yogurt
Salt and pepper, to taste

Accompaniment
2 lb. small boiled or steamed buttered potatoes

Marinate the fillets in garlic, wine, salt, and pepper for 40 minutes.
Roll the fillets and arrange close together, in a greased baking pan and bake at 350 degrees F for 25 minutes or until done.

Sauce
Meanwhile in a saucepan, combine the white wine, onion, garlic, and hot pepper and cook until reduced by half. Add the bell peppers and sugar and cook for 5 more minutes. Let it cool and, together with the yogurt, put through the blender to form a smooth sauce. Adjust salt and pepper. Reheat just before serving.

To Serve
Arrange the fillets on a platter with the boiled potatoes alongside and pour the hot sauce over.
Serves 6.

Peixe com Molho de Azedinha e Erva Doce
Fish with Sorrel and Fennel Sauce

This dish is as attractive as it is delicious, and the cook can prepare the sauce while the fish bakes in the oven. Serve with white rice.

4 6-oz. lean, white fish fillets
Salt and pepper
1 tbsp. olive oil
1 cup white wine

Stock
Fennel fronds
2 cups water
1 medium onion, chopped
12 branches parsley
½ tsp. ground black pepper

Sauce

1 medium-size fennel bulb, sliced crosswise
2 tbsp. olive oil
6 ripe but firm tomatoes, peeled and seeded, cut in slices
¼ tsp. saffron, crushed
¼ cup heavy cream
2 tbsp. lemon or lime juice
Salt and pepper, to taste
1-2 cups sorrel, finely sliced

Heat the oven to 350 degrees F. Oil a baking pan and arrange the fillets in a single layer. Season with salt, pepper, olive oil, and white wine. Cover with aluminum foil and marinate while preparing the stock.

When ready, bake the fish, still covered with aluminum foil, for 15 minutes or until done.

Stock

Combine the fennel fronds, water, onion, parsley, and black pepper in a pan. Bring to a boil, then lower the heat and simmer for 10 minutes. Take off the fire, cool to lukewarm, strain, and return to the pan. Reduce by half, take off the fire, and reserve.

Sauce

Sauté the fennel slices in olive oil for 10 minutes, then add the tomatoes, stock, saffron, cream, lemon juice, salt, and pepper. Cook until thickened, about 5 minutes.

Remove the fish from the oven and pour the liquid from the baking pan into the sauce. Add the sorrel, bring to a boil, and cook until the sorrel is wilted.

To Serve

Arrange the fillets on a platter. Top with some of the sauce and strew the remainder alongside.

Serves 4.

Bacalhau Grelhado com Pesto de Coentro
Fresh Cod with Cilantro Pesto

This pesto, an example of the influence of Italian immigrants on Brazilian cuisine, is lighter than the more familiar basil/pine nut version and perfectly suited to fresh cod, a fish that has always been a favorite of the Portuguese and their descendants.

Pesto
1½ cups fresh cilantro, firmly packed
1 cup parsley, firmly packed
5 cloves garlic, peeled
½ cup walnuts, chopped
½ cup grated Parmesan cheese
¼ tsp. salt
½ cup salad oil

Fish
3 tbsp. olive oil
4 3-4-oz. cod fillets, or other mild, lean white fish

Pesto
Wash and dry both the cilantro and parsley. Using only the leaves, process in a blender or a food processor with garlic, walnuts, cheese, salt, and salad oil. Pulse until pesto becomes a paste not too thin.

Fish
Heat the oil in a frying pan and sauté the fish for 5 minutes or until it is uniformly cooked. Serve topped with the pesto and garnish with sprigs of cilantro.

Serves 4.

Bacalhoada
Codfish Casserole

One glaring absence from any fishmonger's stand is *bacalhãu*, or salt cod, which is never sold with fresh fish. From earliest colonial days when it was brought from Portugal, *bacalhãu* has been featured significantly in the

Brazilian diet, and today it is almost impossible to find a São Paulo restaurant that does not offer it in some form. It is always expensive but particularly so at Easter when Brazilian families traditionally serve it. This recipe will need no added salt, as the fish is salty.

1½ lb. salted codfish, without skin, cut in thick slices
2 large onions
2 large tomatoes
2 cloves garlic
1 green pepper
1 red pepper
1 cup black olives, pitted
2 lb. potatoes
Black pepper, to taste
¼ cup olive oil
2 tbsp. chopped parsley

Put the fish in a large bowl, add water to cover, and refrigerate for 24 hours, changing the water 5 times.

Cut the onions and tomatoes in thick slices. Mince the garlic. Seed the peppers and cut in cubes. Cut the olives lengthwise into quarters if large, or halves if small. Set aside. Peel the potatoes and place in pot with enough water to cover, bring to a boil, and simmer for 10 minutes or until they are almost soft. Drain, cool, and cut into ½-inch slices.

To another pot add the desalted codfish and cover with water. Bring to a high boil and boil for 10 minutes. Drain.

Preheat oven to 350 degrees F. Place the fish in a single layer in a casserole dish and add all the other ingredients except olive oil and parsley. Drizzle with oil, sprinkle with parsley, cover with the lid or foil, and cook in the oven for 45 minutes. Remove the foil and continue to cook for another 15 minutes. Serve hot.

Serves 6.

Baile de Quinua e Camarão
Quinoa and Shrimp Dance

Originally cultivated in the Andes some four thousand years ago, quinoa has been a part of the South American diet ever since that time. However, there has been a recent surge in its popularity in São Paulo with a corresponding number of new recipes. One of them is this light first course, which is ideal when the remainder of the meal is heavier or when the weather is very hot.

⅔ cup quinoa
2 large shrimp
6 asparagus spears
2 scallions
1 tbsp. olive oil
1 tbsp. white wine vinegar
Salt
1 tomato, chopped

Pour enough cold water to cover the quinoa, bring to a boil, and cook for 15 minutes or until done. Bring a separate pot of water to a boil. Drop in the shrimp and boil until done. Then immediately immerse shrimp briefly in ice water to stop the cooking. Steam the asparagus. Slice the scallions and sauté for a few minutes. In a bowl, combine the oil, vinegar, and salt.

When everything is cool, cut the asparagus into 2 inch-pieces, mound the stems in the center of two salad plates, and arrange the tips so that they radiate outward as spokes. Combine the quinoa, scallions, tomatoes, and vinaigrette; mix well; and pile the combination on top of the asparagus stems. Put a shrimp on one side of the mound of quinoa.

Serves 2.

Molho de Camarão para Peixe
Shrimp Sauce for Fish

A little hot red pepper spices up this unusual sauce, which can be used to embellish any mild-flavored white fish.

2 tbsp. olive oil
1 medium onion, chopped
1 small, hot red pepper, minced
1 cup fresh shrimp, cleaned and, if they are large, chopped
½ tsp. nutmeg
1 cup milk
2 tbsp. cornstarch
Salt and pepper, to taste

Sauté the onion, pepper, and shrimp in oil. When shrimp are cooked, add nutmeg and milk. Thicken with cornstarch and season with salt and pepper.

Makes about 2 cups sauce.

Gratiné de Camarão
Gratinéed Shrimp

Like most shrimp dishes, this unusual one undoubtedly came from the state of Bahia. White rice and one of the *farofas* are perfect accompaniments.

1 lb. fresh shrimp
2 large cloves garlic, minced
¼ cup onion, minced
¼ cup soy sauce
1 small hot pepper, seeded and minced
2 tbsp. vegetable oil
1 tomato, peeled and chopped
4 large potatoes, scrubbed, unpeeled, and cut in ½-inch slices
Salt, to taste
4 oz. cream cheese thinned with 2 tbsp. cream, or 4 oz. *requeijão* cheese
Parmesan, freshly grated

Combine the shrimp, garlic, onion, soy sauce, and hot pepper and sauté the mixture in oil. When the shrimp begin to turn pink, add the tomato and sauté on a medium-low fire until the shrimp are done, being careful not to dry out the mixture. Taste for salt. Meanwhile, place the sliced potatoes in a large skillet half filled with salted boiling water and cook until done. Transfer the potato slices to a buttered baking dish and spread the shrimp mixture on top. Cover with cream cheese or *requeijão* and sprinkle generously with Parmesan. Slip under the broiler until the cheese is golden. Alternatively, the dish may be browned in a hot (425 degrees F) oven.

Serves 4.

Cuscuz com Frutos do Mar
Couscous with Seafood

Since more Lebanese live in Brazil than in Lebanon, they may have introduced couscous to this country, although it is also believed that Portuguese immigrants of North African ancestry brought it. While the pasta's true background is unknown, this topping is thoroughly Brazilian and very forgiving. Add less or more of the crab, shrimp, or squid or eliminate one altogether as long as the total amount of seafood weighs in at about 2.5 pounds.

1 lb. squid, cut in rings
1 onion, chopped
2 cloves garlic, chopped

10 oz. crab meat
1 lb. medium-size shrimp
7 oz. bottle coconut milk
3 ripe tomatoes, chopped
14 oz. couscous
2 qt. fish stock
¼ cup parsley, chopped

Scald the squid in boiling water for 2 minutes. In a skillet, sauté the onion and garlic, add the crab and shrimp, and cook for 10 minutes. Add the scalded squid, coconut milk, and chopped tomatoes and cook until the tomatoes are slightly thick. Meanwhile, bring the stock to a boil, take it off the fire, stir in the couscous, cover, and let sit for 10 minutes. Serve the seafood over the couscous. Garnish with chopped parsley.

Serves 6-8.

Camarão com Polenta e Gorgonzola
Shrimp with Polenta and Gorgonzola

Gorgonzola, when cooked, loses much of its bite but none of its unique character and is particularly suited to this dish, which is unusual, quickly prepared, and can be served to both family and guests. Use large but not gigantic shrimp; the original recipe called for the shrimp to be cleaned without removing the tails, a very Brazilian custom. I find this unnecessary and certainly more troublesome, but try it with or without the tails, whichever you like.

Sauce
6 tomatoes, peeled and seeded
1 medium onion, chopped
8 cloves garlic, minced
3 tbsp. olive oil
1 cup parsley, chopped
1 cup scallions, thinly sliced

Gorgonzola Cream
1½ cups light cream or half-and-half
4 oz. Gorgonzola

Polenta
1 cup quick-cook cornmeal
¼ cup butter
Salt and pepper, to taste

Shrimp
¼ cup olive oil
22-25 large shrimp, cleaned
Toasted pine nuts

Sauce
Chop the tomatoes. Sauté the onion and ½ the garlic in a few spoonfuls of olive oil until translucent, then add the tomatoes and cook for 5 minutes or until thickened. Add the parsley and scallions.

Gorgonzola Cream

Boil the cream until reduced by half and add the crumbled gorgonzola, stirring to make a smooth cream.

Polenta

Cook the cornmeal as directed on the package, adding the butter to the water, stirring constantly. Add salt and pepper to taste. Keep warm.

Shrimp

In a large skillet, sauté the remaining garlic in olive oil, add the shrimp, and sauté until just done, seasoning with salt and pepper.

To Serve

If necessary, reheat the tomato sauce. Make a bed of gorgonzola cream on a platter and top with the hot cornmeal and then the shrimp. Pour the tomato sauce over all. Sprinkle with toasted pine nuts.

Serves 6.

Sopa de Camarão
Shrimp Soup

Peanut butter is unknown in Brazil, and when I was given this recipe, it included roasted peanuts, ground in the blender with the tomato mixture. I found this slightly gritty and successfully replaced the nuts with smooth peanut butter, which I had purchased on a visit to the U.S.

2 cups chicken stock
2 cups fish stock
2 small chili peppers, minced
2 tbsp. grated fresh ginger
8 tomatoes, peeled, seeded, and chopped
2 cups coconut milk
3 tbsp. smooth peanut butter with only salt added
1 lb. small or medium shrimp, peeled and cleaned
¼ cup lemon or lime juice
Salt, to taste
¼ cup cilantro, chopped

Combine the two stocks, peppers, ginger, and tomatoes in a large pot and simmer for 10 minutes. Cool to lukewarm. Add the coconut milk and peanut butter and whirl the soup in the blender until smooth. Return the soup to the pan and heat to a simmer. Add the shrimp and lemon juice and cook for 5 more minutes. Add salt to taste and garnish with cilantro.

Serves 8.

Camarões com Mamão Verde
Shrimp with Green Papaya

Whenever cooking papaya, be sure the exterior is very green or the fruit will turn to mush when heated.

1 large papaya (about 2 lb.)
3 tbsp. butter or margarine
10 oz. medium to large shrimp, cleaned and peeled
1 tbsp. sugar
Juice of 2 large lemons
Salt and pepper, to taste

Peel the papaya and cut crosswise in ½- to ¾-inch slices. Carefully remove the seeds, keeping the slices in one piece. In a large skillet, melt 1 tbsp. butter and sauté the slices over medium-low heat, turning them to brown both sides. Remove and reserve.

Raise the flame to medium and, in the same pan, melt another tbsp. butter and sauté the shrimp, turning once. Remove when they are firm and colored.

Over a very low fire, add the sugar to the same pan and allow it to melt and caramelize. This doesn't take long. Immediately add the lemon juice and stir constantly to dissolve the melted sugar. Season with salt and pepper and add remaining butter. Return the papaya and shrimp to the pan, heat, and serve.

Serves 4.

Bobo de Camarão
Shrimp *Bobo*

This is a classic, traditional Brazilian dish. Originating in the north, the coconut milk, hot peppers, manioc, and fresh shrimp show the African influence on the cuisine of the country. If manioc is not locally available in markets selling Latin American foodstuffs, mashed potatoes may be substituted, and it will still be delicious although not as authentic. *Dendê* oil is available through the same markets that offer manioc.

2 lb. fresh manioc (*mandioca*), peeled and quartered
Salt, to taste
3 tbsp. olive oil
1 onion, chopped
2 cloves garlic, minced
3 tomatoes, chopped
1 green pepper, chopped
2 lb. medium to large shrimp, cleaned
2 tbsp. cilantro, finely chopped
1 cup coconut milk
Salt, to taste
1 tsp. *dendê* oil (optional)

Cook the manioc in a large pot with water to cover until tender. Remove the central cord and put through the blender, adding water as needed to make a purée. Taste for salt and reserve.

Sauté the onion and garlic in olive oil; when translucent, add the tomatoes and green pepper and cook for about 5 minutes. Add the shrimp and cilantro and cook over low heat until the shrimp are done. Add the coconut milk and dendê oil, if using; mix well; and taste for salt. Stir in the manioc and serve immediately with white rice.

Serves 6.

Camarão com Maracujá e Coco na Minimoranga
Shrimp with Passion Fruit and Coconut in a Mini-Squash

Brazilians are fond of serving various kinds of stews in large squash, but this very easy shrimp dish is often served in individual mini-squashes. In this case, each person scoops out some of the cooked squash along with the shrimp and sauce. Although it's an elegant and impressive presentation, small squash are not easily located, and this dish is just as tasty when served in a winter squash. Winter squash (acorn, butternut, or Hubbard) can be steamed or baked then mashed and can become a bed for the shrimp and sauce.

4 small squashes, or 2 lb. winter squash
Fish stock
1½ lb. shrimp, cleaned
4 passion fruit (to make ⅓ cup juice)
2 tbsp. butter
2 tbsp. vegetable oil
⅓ cup flour
2 cups fish stock
½ cup coconut milk
Salt and pepper

If squash are used whole, cut the top as a lid, scoop out the seeds, and pour in about ¼ cup fish stock. Replace the top, and bake at 350 degrees F for about 45 minutes. When done, remove the top, pour out the stock, and fill with shrimp and sauce. If winter squash is to be mashed, cut it in large pieces, remove the seeds and strings, and steam until tender. Discard the skin and mash as for mashed potatoes.

Cut the passion fruit in half, scrape the seeds and pulp into the blender, and blend for a few seconds on medium speed. Strain, discard the seeds, and reserve ⅓ cup of the pulp/juice. (Since it is impossible to know in advance how much juice each fruit will yield, it's better to have too much than too little. Any excess can be frozen for future use or mixed with orange juice, yogurt, and honey for a tropical smoothie.)

While the squash cooks, take a large skillet and sauté the shrimp in butter and oil until it loses transparency. Remove and reserve. Stir flour into the remaining butter and oil and gradually add the 2 cups of stock, coconut milk, and passion fruit juice, stirring over a low fire until thickened and free of lumps. Return shrimp to this sauce, adjust the seasoning, and stir well.

If using small squashes, divide the shrimp and sauce among them, propping the "lid" attractively against the side of the squash. If using mashed winter squash, serve the squash and shrimp in separate bowls, ladling the shrimp over each serving of squash.

Serves 4.

Lula Recheada
Stuffed Squid

The amount of everything but the squid, tuna, and red pepper in this easy supper dish depends on the size of the squid, which should be medium to large. Remember that squid shrink when sautéed, so they should not be stuffed to overflowing.

4 whole squid, cleaned inside and out
3 oz. tuna (½ of 6 oz. can)
2 tbsp. chopped red bell pepper
Red onion, chopped
Capers, chopped
Garlic, chopped
Scallions, chopped
Parsley, chopped
Salt and pepper, to taste
2 tbsp. oil

Combine all the ingredients but the squid and the oil, mix well, and stuff the squid with the mixture. Close the openings with toothpicks and sauté in oil, over low heat until done. Serve with mashed potatoes.
Serves 2.

Salada de Lulas e Cítricos
Squid and Citrus Salad

Grapefruit are not grown in Brazil, so this salad is considered exotic and chic. Choose small squid, cut them into thin rings, and they will cook very quickly and be quite tender. Use the tentacles as well.

2 tbsp. vegetable oil
¾ lb. squid, cleaned and cut into rings
6 tbsp. sugar
2 tbsp. water
¼ cup rice vinegar
½ tsp. Asian chili sauce (Sriracha, aka "rooster sauce," or similar), or to taste
5 tbsp. oil
Salt, to taste
1 large orange, peeled and sectioned
1 grapefruit, peeled and sectioned
12 mint leaves, chopped
8 cups assorted lettuce, including radicchio, torn into bite-size pieces

Heat the vegetable oil and quickly sauté the squid rings. Be careful not to overcook or they will toughen. Cool and chill. For the vinaigrette, combine the sugar and water in a saucepan and cook for 5 minutes over low heat. Cool to room temperature, add the vinegar, chili sauce, oil, and salt and beat to blend. Chill. In a bowl, combine the orange, grapefruit, and mint leaves and chill. At serving time, toss the assorted lettuce leaves with some of the dressing and pile onto individual plates. Toss the citrus/mint mixture with more dressing, mound on top of the leaves, and then arrange the squid on top.

Serves 4.

3

Fruit

By mid-morning, the feira is teeming with shoppers and noisy with venders shouting their wares. For the last hour or so, the market has been threaded with *carregadores*. These are boys from the nearby *favelas* (slums) and *cortiços* (tenements) who earn money pulling carts and carrying bags for feira customers through the market and then on to the patron's homes or cars. Polite, dressed in clean, if threadbare clothing, they usually earn one real (about fifty-six U.S. cents) from each patron. They don't earn very much, but it helps their families. Shoppers receive offers from several hopeful *carregadores* who call women *Tia*, or Auntie, as they ask the inevitable question, "Auntie, do you want a *carregador?*" Often, potential customers will decline the request, but they will, instead, offer to buy the boy a *pastel* and a cup of *caldo de cana*. It is a proposal that is never turned down.

In every feira there is at least one flimsy stand with a counter on three sides and metal stools that are always filled with customers eating plump *pasteis*, large squares of pastry dough filled with cheese, shrimp, or dried meat, doubled over, and deep-fried by a cook on the other side of the counter. *Pasteis* are a national passion as is *caldo de cana*, or sugar-cane juice. Every feira has a stand where juice is squeezed from sugar canes as the latter are fed into an apparatus that resembles an old-fashioned washing machine wringer. Customers may buy large or small cups with or without lime juice.

Fruit stands abound at the feiras, and at each stand, samples are pressed upon potential clients. A slice of pineapple impaled on a knife, followed by a generous portion of mango, section of orange, slice of apple, guava, and perhaps half a *pinha* nestled in a small sheet of wax paper are consumed by discerning shoppers as the stand owner implores them to test even more of his wares and, above all, buy. Tasting of the wares is an old feature of Brazilian street life and travel agents have found it necessary to warn Brazilian clients headed for the U.S. that they may not sample at will when marketing abroad.

On the fruit stands, shiny scarlet apples are polished and stacked in two perfect pyramids according to variety; pears are partially wrapped in tissue paper and aligned in rows; large, purple grapes, weighed into kilo (2.2 pounds) portions, rest on cellophane nests; and guavas are clinically aligned. Figs, strawberries, and *pinha* are extraordinarily fragile and remain in their original, small boxes, although tipped up on one end for display purposes.

Our favorite stand in the Sunday Praça Roosevelt market is owned by João, a short, calm man of about fifty who has worked in the feira for the past thirty-three years. This particular stand has existed since 1952 and originally belonged to his father-in-law, but, like many of the feira workers, João's children do not intend to follow him into this profession. One son who has recently graduated from college in physical education is employed as a swimming instructor, specializing in young children, while the other, still a student, intends to become a pharmacist.

Ideally, stand owners buy high-quality, low-cost produce nightly, always from the market in Serra da Cantareira or CEAGSP (Companhia Entrepostos e Armazéns Gerais de São Paulo). Like most of his colleagues, João can infallibly predict the number of days it will take for any green item to ripen and willingly selects requested merchandise, although clients are always free to choose their own.

Pineapple. Originating in Central America, *abacaxi*, known in the U.S. as pineapple, has an illustrious history. A pineapple was offered to Christopher Columbus when he arrived in Guadalupe as a gesture of welcome and goodwill. In England, called the Queen of Fruits, it was considered a true

model of beauty and exoticism and was offered to royal guests as a symbol of hospitality. Reputedly bringing good luck, pineapples made of ceramic, stone, and silver are often found on Brazilian gate pillars and as decorations. The fruit contains an interesting enzyme, bromelain, which is a meat tenderizer but also digests milk proteins, severely limiting its use in desserts, particularly those calling for gelatin.

Pineapples, or *abacaxis*, are grown in profusion in Brazil, but expertise is usually required in picking a ripe, juicy one, as it depends on the color, weight, and feel of the fruit rather than the aroma or easily plucked fronds. When João, like his colleagues, assesses a pineapple, he tosses it gently from hand to hand, scrutinizes the color, and turns it upside down before pronouncing it ripe. And it is always perfectly delicious. Slices of pineapple, a popular snack, are sold on São Paulo street corners from little carts that usually offer a few other fruits as well.

Abacaxi de Gala
Pineapple Shells with Shrimp Filling

Because this can be prepared well in advance, *Abacaxi de Gala* is a perfect luncheon or buffet dish, though it is also welcome for dinner on a hot day. For a very Brazilian meal, start with Marinated Zucchini and end with *Crème de Papaya*.

12 oz. shrimp, cleaned
Lime juice
Salt and pepper
2 tbsp. olive oil
1 tsp. crushed garlic
1 ripe pineapple
1 ½ cups heavy cream
1 tsp. mustard
1 14-oz. jar palmito, sliced in medium rounds
2 onions, finely chopped

Season the shrimp with lime juice, salt, and pepper. In a pan, heat the oil and sauté the garlic. Drain the shrimp and add them to the pan. Sauté, remove, and cool. Cut the pineapple in half lengthwise, scoop out the pulp, being careful not to break the shell, and cut the flesh in cubes. In a bowl, delicately mix together the pineapple, cream, mustard, slices of palmito, and chopped onion. Season with salt and pepper and add the cooled shrimp. Fill the pineapple halves and place on a platter decorated with the pineapple fronds.

Serves 6.

Sorvete de Abacaxi
Pineapple Ice Cream

This is another recipe where the shell may be used as a serving dish, although I usually prepare the ice cream and keep it shell-less in the freezer. The directions here are for presenting it in the shell, probably for a special occasion or a summer dinner party.

1 ripe, medium-size pineapple
2 qt. vanilla ice cream

Cut the pineapple in half lengthwise and save both halves, including the fronds. With a metal spoon and a small knife, remove the pineapple pulp and chop roughly. Cook it in a saucepan over a low fire for about 30 minutes or until it is golden, stirring frequently so that the pineapple doesn't stick to the pan. Remove from the fire and cool completely. When the pineapple is absolutely cold, soften the ice cream and quickly combine with the cooked pineapple. Stuff the reserved shells. Freeze until serving time.

Serves 8.

Abacaxi e Ricota Torte
Pineapple and Ricotta Pie

This crust is closer to cookie dough than a pie crust, is considerably thicker when rolled out, and doesn't need the delicate handling that a pie crust requires. Do not try to double the dough and lift it into the pie plate after rolling it out, as this will not work. Instead, roll the dough out on wax paper, invert the pie plate over the dough, and, with the help of the wax paper, flip the plate, dough, and paper over. You can then remove the paper and fit the dough into the pie plate.

Fruit

Dough

4 cups flour
1 cup butter
¾ cup sugar
1 egg
2 egg whites
1 tsp. baking powder

Filling

1 pineapple
1 cup and 2 tbsp. sugar
1 tsp. cornstarch
8 oz. ricotta cheese
2 eggs
½ cup milk
1 tsp. vanilla extract
½ cup Brazil nuts, chopped

Dough

Mix all the dough ingredients first with a fork and then with the fingers, wrap in plastic wrap, and refrigerate for 1 hour.

Filling

Cut the pineapple in half and scoop out the fruit, discarding the hard core. Chop the fruit into fairly fine pieces; you should have about 3 cups of fruit. Mix with 1 cup of sugar in a saucepan, cover, and cook over a low fire, stirring from time to time, in order to dissolve the sugar and soften the pineapple. Remove from the fire and, when it is lukewarm, beat in the blender. Return it to the pan, add the cornstarch, mix well, and cook over a low fire for about 5 minutes or until it is transparent. Remove from the fire and cool.

While it is cooling, beat the ricotta, eggs, milk, and vanilla in the blender. Reserve.

Remove the dough from the refrigerator, roll it out on wax paper, and fit it in a 10-inch pie pan as explained above. Spread with the pineapple, top with the ricotta cream, and sprinkle with chopped nuts. Bake at 350 degrees F for about 30 minutes or until the crust is golden and the filling has set. Cool and chill.

Serves 8.

Pinha Colada Brasileira
Brazilian Pinha Colada

Although known in the U.S. as a drink, this version is a pineapple dessert. *Cachaça*, Brazilian sugar-cane alcohol, is sold in most large liquor stores in the U.S. If you can't find it in your area, light rum (which is also made here from fermented sugar cane) may be substituted.

1 medium-size pineapple
¼ cup *doce de leite**
½ cup *cachaça* or light rum
2 cups orange juice
½ tsp. vanilla extract

To remove the pineapple shell, cut off a ¾-inch slice from the top, including fronds, stand the pineapple upright, and make downward strokes with a sharp knife, removing the shell in strips. To remove the "eyes," make shallow diagonal cuts in the form of a "v." Turn the pineapple on its side and cut off the bottom part of the shell. You now have a pineapple with only fruit and no shell or eyes.

Melt the *doce de leite* in a pot large enough to hold the pineapple. When it bubbles and is on the point of caramelizing, add the pineapple and pour the *cachaça* over. Add the orange juice and bring to a boil, then lower the heat, and cook uncovered for 30 minutes, turning the pineapple every 5 minutes or so to cook evenly. Take off the fire and stir the vanilla into the sauce. Cool and then chill in the cooking liquid, which is now the sauce.

To serve, cut the pineapple in thick slices accompanied by either coconut or vanilla ice cream. Pass the sauce separately.

Serves 8.
Refer to the sources guide or check the Latino market in your area

Passion fruit. *Maracujá,* known in the U.S. as passion fruit, originated in Brazil, where it is considered nature's tranquilizer. One of its most notable features are the flowers, so beautiful that missionaries in Brazil saw this as a true present from God to illuminate the Catechism and explain the history of the Passion of Christ to the indigenous. They imagined the floral crown transformed into the actual image of the crown of thorns; the three stigmas of the flowers as the three nails pinning Christ to the cross, and the five antlers as the beating received by the martyred Christ. To them, the round fruit represented the world that Christ came to save; therefore, the flowers and fruits of this vine were called the Passion of Christ.

Maracujá doce, sweet passion fruit, is oval in shape, smooth, yellow, and a cousin of the common passion fruit, but it is more expensive and difficult to find. Stand vendors rarely carry them because of the price, but they can often be found in upscale markets. They are not cooked but sliced in half lengthwise, and both transparent flesh and seeds are eaten raw with a spoon.

Help is never needed to determine ripeness when buying the common passion fruit. After weighing each piece of fruit in cupped hands, it is shaken close to one ear. Passion fruit should be heavy and if there is any rattle within the firm shell, it means the fruit is drying up and past its prime.

For most uses, including juice, the pulp should be separated from the seeds by cutting the fruit in half, spooning the contents into a blender, and blending briefly before pressing through a strainer with a wooden spoon. Because the quantity of fluid in each piece of fruit is completely unpredictable, these recipes call for measured amounts of strained juice rather than a specific number of *maracujá*. When the fresh fruit is unavailable, bottled unsweetened juice may be substituted.

Pudim com Maracujá
Caramel Pudding with Passion Fruit

These puddings are really miniature caramel custards raised to gastronomic elegance through the surrounding pool of heavy cream and *maracujá* pulp. This is a very rich dessert, so it's best to choose ceramic molds that hold a four-ounce capacity and fill them to the top. Accompany with simple sugar or ginger cookies or serve alone.

1 cup water
1 cup sugar
1 cup white wine
1½ cups sugar
2 eggs
5 egg yolks
1¼ cups heavy cream or half-and-half
1½ cups *maracujá* pulp, spooned from the shell

Fruit

In a pot, combine the water and 1 cup sugar and boil until the mixture is golden brown. Immediately pour into eight small ramekins, tilting to coat the sides. In a saucepan, reduce the wine by half and cool. Mix the sugar, eggs, egg yolks, cooled wine, and cream. Pour into the prepared molds and bake in a pan with boiling water reaching halfway up the sides of the ramekins for about 45 minutes at 350 degrees F. Do not overcook. When a table knife inserted in the center of a pudding comes out clean, remove from the oven and immediately transfer the custards from the pan of hot water to one of cold. Chill in the refrigerator for several hours or overnight. To serve, unmold on individual plates. Pour heavy cream on one side of the pudding and unstrained passion fruit pulp, including the seeds, on the other.

Serves 8.

Musse de Maracujá
Passion Fruit Mousse

There are endless variations of this classic dessert, and, at one point, I felt that I had tested most of them. Some are delicious but use raw eggs, both the whites and heavy cream beaten stiff and then combined with the other ingredients. The one I chose is very traditional and has only four components—gelatin, condensed milk, fresh passion fruit juice, and heavy cream. Don't be afraid to experiment with this recipe—it's not like baking a cake where every measurement should be exact. You may prefer more juice, less cream, maybe less or more gelatin, or perhaps just as it is here, but it is virtually impossible to ruin it.

1 envelope gelatin
Cold water
Hot water
Passion fruit juice
1 14-oz. can sweetened condensed milk
1 cup heavy cream

In a small cup, soak the gelatin in cold water for a few minutes, then dissolve over hot water. Prepare the juice, first blending briefly and straining out the seeds. You will need the same amount of juice and condensed milk. Beat the juice and milk together and gradually add the cream and gelatin. Continue beating to incorporate all the ingredients and pour into a glass serving dish or individual serving dishes. Chill for several hours until very cold.

Serves 6.

Creme Brule de Maracujá
Crème Brûlée with Passion Fruit

The tartness of passion fruit lightens this custard and lends an intriguing and unusual flavor to the dish.

2 cups heavy cream
2 large eggs
2 large egg yolks
¾ cup sugar
1 cup strained purée of passion-fruit juice

Heat the cream until very warm. Beat eggs and yolks and blend in sugar and purée. Slowly add warm cream to egg mixture and mix gently to dissolve the sugar. Pour into the ramekins and put them in a baking or roasting pan. Pour hot water into the baking pan until it reaches halfway up the sides of the ramekins and bake at 350 degrees F for approximately 1 hour or until a

table knife comes out nearly clean. The cream will still jiggle in the middle but will firm up. Briefly immerse the ramekins in cold water to stop the cooking process and then cool on a rack. Chill custards for up to two days.

Remove from refrigerator and sprinkle each ramekin with 2 tsp. of sugar. Place ramekins in oven with preheated broiler 3 inches above ramekins to caramelize the sugar or use a kitchen blowtorch for this final touch.

Serves 6.

Mangoes, or *mangas,* as they are known in Portuguese, can always be found in the feira, but João offers only the better varieties—usually Keitt, Tommy, Palmer, or Haden—out of a total of the twenty-seven grown in Brazil. Not indigenous to Brazil, this fruit was originally grown in India, a country that is still their number one exporter. Although, around 1700, the Portuguese brought mangoes to the state of Bahia, today São Paulo and neighboring Minas Gerais produce 25 percent of the country's total output. Belem is known for its mangoes, as is Rio de Janeiro, which has named one of its most famous samba schools Mangueira, after this fruit.

Mangoes in Brazil are green or orange and do not change color when ripe. The latter stage is detected by a very slight softness of the flesh when pressed, and when past their prime, they develop dark spots. Mangoes are one of the most popular fruits in Brazil and are eaten raw or cooked in an infinite number of ways; aprons are mandatory when cutting this fruit as they stain badly.

Creme Brule com Manga
Crème Brûlée with Mango

Here is another Brazilian version of classic crème brûlée; it is unusual, delicious, and ideal for dinner parties since it must be made well in advance. The straight-sided, white ceramic cups that look like miniature soufflé dishes are best for this dish; the brûlée bakes evenly and the white tone sets off the bronzed sugar crust.

6 egg yolks
⅓ cup and 1 tbsp. sugar
¾ tsp. vanilla extract
1 cup heavy cream
1 cup milk

Fresh mango cut in small cubes
2 tbsp. or more sugar, to cover the crème

Thoroughly mix the yolks, sugar, and vanilla. In a saucepan, bring the milk and cream to a boil and slowly add to the eggs. Distribute the mango pieces in 6 ceramic ramekins, measuring 3 inches across and 2 ¼ inches high,* and pour the cream over. Bake in a pan with boiling water reaching halfway up the sides of the ramekins at 350 degrees F for 45 minutes to 1 hour or until a table knife inserted in the center comes out clean. Cool, then chill. Just before serving, sprinkle sugar generously on the surface and caramelize under a very hot grill or with a kitchen blowtorch.

Serves 6-8 depending on the cup size used.
*Use eight cups if you prefer to use the smaller size.

Manga Grelhada
Sautéed Mango

This light first course, with a sauce reflecting the cuisine of immigrants from the Middle East, takes the place of a salad or soup.

Fruit

1 mango
½ tbsp. black sesame seeds
½ tbsp. white sesame seeds
1 cup (or more) alfalfa sprouts
1 tbsp. butter

Sauce
1 tbsp. *tahine*
4 tbsp. cold water
2 tbsp. lemon or lime juice
Salt, to taste

Peel the mango and cut it in half laterally. In a bowl, mix the sesame seeds together and press them into the mango so that they adhere well. Using the alfalfa sprouts, make a nest on 2 salad plates.

Melt the butter in a skillet and quickly sauté the mangos on both sides, then remove and arrange in the alfalfa nests. Beat all the sauce ingredients together and spoon over the mango.

Serves 2.

Prosciutto, Manga e Parmesão
Prosciutto, Mango, and Parmesan

This is another first course replacement for soup or salad. The Parmesan must be fresh and in shards, which can be shaved with a vegetable peeler or the side of a grater.

1-2 mangoes
4 oz. prosciutto
Parmesan shards

Peel the mangoes and slice into ½-inch slices. Arrange on salad plates, cover with prosciutto, and scatter parmesan on top.

Serves 4.

Pudim de Chocolate Branco com Pimenta Rosa e Molho de Manga
White Chocolate Flan with Pink Peppercorns and Mango Sauce

Requeijão is an enormously popular soft, white, creamy cheese that was developed by Brazilian immigrant Mario Silvestrini in 1911; it can be found in some markets listed in the sources section. Strawberries can be successfully substituted for the mangos in the sauce.

    2 tsp. plain gelatin
    1 tbsp. water
    1½ cups cream
    1 cup *requeijão* cheese, or cream cheese mixed with 1 tbsp. sour cream
    2 tsp. ground pink peppercorns
    7 oz. white chocolate

Sauce
5½ cups ripe mango, peeled and cut in pieces
2 tbsp. confectioner's sugar

Soften the gelatin in 1 tbsp. water and dissolve over hot water. Set aside. In a saucepan, bring the cream, *requeijão* cheese, and peppercorns to a boil. Turn off the heat and add the white chocolate, stirring until melted and well mixed. Add the gelatin. Stir again. Pour into 6 ramekins and refrigerate for 2-3 hours or more.

Sauce
Place the cut up mango and the sugar in a blender and mix until it becomes a thick sauce. To serve, divide the sauce among the plates and unmold the flans on top of the sauce. Decorate with white chocolate shavings and a piece of mango.

Serves 6-8 depending on the size of the ramekins.

Sopa Gelada de Frutas Tropicais
Cold Tropical Fruit Soup

Juice bars, where all imaginable combinations of fresh fruit are turned into delectable drinks, attest to the Brazilian love of juice. From these drinks, there is a short step to a chilled fruit soup, such as this delicious one, which should be served on a very hot day.

1 large pineapple, peeled and cored
4 ripe mangoes, peeled and pitted
2 tbsp. crushed papaya pulp
¼ cup additional pineapple juice
1 tbsp. orange zest
1 tbsp. rum
2 cups milk
2 cups cream

Place all the ingredients except milk and cream in the blender and purée. Strain to remove fibers, pressing on the sieve to extract all the juice. Slowly mix in milk and cream and chill for 4-5 hours.

Serves 6-8.

Papaya. Native to the tropics of South America, papaya is produced year-round and, together with the banana, is the most widely consumed fruit in Brazil. Although papaya was not grown commercially until thirty or forty years ago, it is now a major export. Unlike the vast majority of fruit trees, male and female papaya trees are separate, and the male's principal function is to fertilize the flowers of the female. Occasionally, however, the flowers are hermaphrodites, and in these cases the fruits are atypical.

There are many varieties of papaya in Brazil, and they range in size from five inches to the sixteen-inch *mamão*. When ripe, their green skin turns yellow and the flesh becomes a deep pink. Commonly, Brazilians eat halves of this fruit, along with the seeds, for breakfast and frequently as a snack. It also appears in main dishes, vegetables, soups, and desserts, both cooked and raw. The fruit contains papain, an enzyme that acts as a meat tenderizer, aids in human digestion, and lowers cholesterol. The seeds have a medicinal use both as an antiworm remedy and a treatment for cirrhosis of the liver.

According to a few models in Brazil, papaya is wonderful for the complexion. To eliminate wrinkles, they suggest scraping out the flesh until white latex liquid runs free and pressing the prepared papaya skin against the face for twenty minutes. Experts have, however, warned that the enzyme can burn sensitive skin, so wise Brazilians have decided to forgo this beauty treatment of doubtful success.

There are, however, a multitude of bona fide industrial and medicinal uses for this fruit, ranging from the treatment of gastric problems to use as a leather and wool softener.

Crème de Papaia
Cream of Papaya with Cassis

This dessert took São Paulo by storm some twenty years ago, moving papaya from a breakfast treat to the dinner table, and it now appears on the menus of all the top restaurants in the city. It may also be made with a large mango rather than the papaya or, more rarely, with strawberries. In any case, don't worry about exact proportions of the first two ingredients, which may be adjusted to individual tastes. The cassis is essential but only threaded delicately on top; this is a case where too much will overwhelm the dessert.

1 small ripe papaya, peeled, seeded, and cut in cubes
1 large scoop vanilla ice cream
1 tbsp. cassis liqueur (more or less)

Beat the papaya cubes and ice cream in the blender at high speed until it is smooth and reaches the consistency of heavy cream. Immediately pour into an individual serving bowl, drizzle with cassis, and decorate with a spray of mint leaves.

Serves 1.

Papaia Oxum
Oxum's Papaya

Oxum, the goddess of love, intimacy, beauty, and wealth, was brought to Brazil by African slaves and is an integral part of the Candomblé religion today. Her color is yellow, she is generous and kind, and this unusual side dish was probably created in her honor by one of Oxum's followers. Best served with any roasted meat, chicken, or fish, the papaya must be uniformly green on the exterior.

2 green papaya (1-1½ lb. each)
1¼ cups unsweetened coconut, grated
½ cup dried shrimp, rinsed
2 tbsp. chopped cilantro
1 large onion, chopped
2 tsp. *dendê* oil (optional)
Salt
1 hot chili pepper, minced

Peel the papaya, cut in half, and remove the seeds. Cut into large pieces and steam for 10 minutes. Cut the papaya into bite-sized cubes, combine with all the other ingredients, and cook. Add water as needed, until the papaya is tender.

Serves 6.

Avocado. Indigenous to Central America, the avocado, or *abacate*, is now popular worldwide. Although there are more than one hundred varieties of this fruit, the one most commonly found in Brazil is slightly larger than a softball and has a much milder flavor than those usually found in the U.S. Perhaps for this reason, Brazilians primarily use it in desserts, unlike Americans who treat it as a vegetable, tossing it into salads, whipping it into soup, and using it as the basis for guacamole. A popular dessert here is mashed avocado, sweetened with a great deal of sugar and flavored with a bit of port. It is definitely not my favorite, but if you decide to try it, be sure to use white port or none at all; ruby port will result in a very unpleasant color.

This fruit was popular with the Aztecs—who called it *ahuacatl*—and also with the Mayans. In the latter civilization, it was known as *oiluacacuahuitl*, which also means testicles, presumably due to its shape.

Palmito com Abacate
Hearts of Palm and Avocado with Passion Fruit Dressing

This is a wonderful salad featuring two very Brazilian ingredients: heart of palm and passion fruit.

½ cup olive oil
1 tbsp. lime juice
½ tsp. white wine vinegar
1½ tsp. sugar
Pinch salt
1 tbsp. red onion, finely chopped
½ cup purée of passion fruit
1 tbsp. parsley, finely chopped
12 cups bite-size pieces of lettuce
8 hearts of palm, cut in ¼-inch slices
2 avocados, cubed
Black pepper

Mix the olive oil, lime juice, white wine vinegar, sugar, salt, red onion, passion fruit, and parsley in a bowl and reserve. Toss the lettuce, hearts of palm, and avocado in a salad bowl and drizzle with the passion fruit dressing. Toss again carefully and add a grinding of black pepper.

Serves 6.

Sorvete de Abacate
Avocado Ice Cream

This delicate ice cream is easy to make and typical of the Brazilian treatment of this fruit. Vodka is added to counteract the tendency of ice creams made with a high proportion of fruit to milk/cream to become very hard and icy in the freezer.

2 lb. avocados, peeled and pitted
½ cup milk
Grated zest of 1 lemon
⅓ cup lemon juice
¼ tsp. salt
1 cup sugar
1 cup heavy cream
3 tbsp. vodka

Cut the avocado flesh coarsely and combine with the milk, lemon zest, lemon juice, and salt in the blender. When smooth, add the sugar, cream, and vodka and blend to amalgamate the ingredients. Process in an ice cream maker.

Makes about 1½ qt.

Guava. Native to South America, *goiaba*, in Brazil, is most commonly used in guava jelly and in a sweet paste known as *goiabada*. Sold in almost every food shop, the latter varies from a firm block to a soft paste; comes in cellophane wrappers, cans, or jars; and is often eaten as a dessert called Romeo and Juliet. In this dessert, a slice of *goiabada* is accompanied by a slice of white cheese from the state of Minas Gerais, which can be closely approximated by using a good-quality, fresh ricotta. Occasionally, the Minas cheese in Romeo and Juliet is replaced by *requeijão*, a soft, white, spreadable Brazilian cheese that can be somewhat duplicated by whipping cream cheese with a spoonful of sour cream.

When ripe, guava have unblemished yellow skin and coral-red flesh. The fruit travels well and are often sold green to ripen within several days. With the most vitamin C of any commercial fruit, the leaves and flowers are used to treat children's intestinal problems. The peel is high in tannin, making it useful in the cosmetic industry in the production of skin products and deodorants.

Suflê de Goiabada
Guava Soufflé

There are several Brazilian guava soufflés of varying interest and culinary difficulty; however, this one is delicious, easy to make, and uses up all those egg whites that are left over from sauces, puddings, and homemade ice cream. The easiest way to keep a supply on hand is to freeze each white separately, using any small container. When each one is frozen, bag it in plastic in the freezer along with the others. Then, when you want to make your soufflé, it's easy to count out the number, put them in a bowl, and defrost at room temperature. This easy recipe was passed to us by a Brazilian friend who especially likes it because it bakes while you eat supper.

8 egg whites
¼ tsp. cream of tartar
½–¾ cup soft guava jam*

Beat the eggs whites, add the cream of tartar, and beat stiff. Add the guava jam and beat stiff again. Grease and flour 1 large soufflé dish and fill with the guava mixture. Bake at 350 degrees F for 30-40 minutes.

Serves 8.

If you are buying this in a specialty or Brazilian market, it is called goiabada mole *or* goiabada cremosa.

Goiabada Suflê com Calda de Requeijão
Guava Soufflé with Cheese Sauce

Similar to the previous Guava Soufflé, this elegant dessert is currently one of the most popular in São Paulo. Both the guava and the cheese, which comes in a glass cup, can be found in most Latino stores or through the sources included at the back of this book. If *requeijão* isn't available, light cream cheese mixed with 1 tbsp. sour cream may be substituted.

Soufflé
4 egg whites
Pinch salt
6 tbsp. soft guava jam or guava paste

Sauce
1 cup *requeijão*
3 tbsp. water

Soufflé
Beat the eggs whites until they form stiff peaks. Add the salt and guava jam and mix very gently. Grease and flour 4 individual soufflé dishes and fill with the guava mixture. Bake at 350 degrees F for 7 minutes or until slightly golden.

Sauce
In a small pan over low heat, melt the cheese with water for 2 minutes. At table, pass the sauce separately. Everyone makes a small hole in their hot soufflé and pours in a little sauce.

Serves 4.

Torta de Goiaba
Guava Tart

Dr. Lenina Pomeranz served this delicious tart for an after-concert supper in her home one evening. The daughter of Polish immigrants, Lenina is the professor of Russian economics and politics at the University of São Paulo, is involved in many academic projects, yet manages to cook both Polish and Brazilian dishes with enthusiasm and expertise.

Dough
1 cup corn starch
2 cups flour
1½ cups sugar
½ cup margarine or butter
½ tsp. baking soda
1 tsp. baking powder
2 eggs
1 tsp. cinnamon
Grated zest of 1 lemon or lime

Filling
11 oz. guava jam (also called *goiabada mole* and *goiabada cremosa*)
Juice of 2 oranges
Juice of 1 lemon or lime

Dough
Lightly mix all the dough ingredients together into a moist meal. Set aside.

Filling
Combine the guava jam, orange juice, and lime juice, beating if necessary to obtain a homogenized paste.

Divide the dough in half, butter an 11- or 12-inch spring-form pan, and cover the bottom with half the dough. Cover with the filling and distribute the remainder of the dough on top. Bake at 350 degrees F for about 40 minutes. Serve at room temperature.

Serves 10-15.

Musse de Queijo com Goiabas
Cheese Mousse with Guavas

This is a rich dessert and an interesting combination of fresh guava and guava jam.

½ lb. cottage cheese or ricotta
7 oz. sour cream
1 can sweetened condensed milk
1 packet gelatin
3 tbsp. rum
1¼ cups heavy cream
Guava jam*
Small slices of fresh guava, without seeds
Sugar

Mix the cottage cheese, sour cream, and condensed milk in the blender. In a small bowl, soak the gelatin in rum for about 5 minutes, then dissolve by putting the bowl of rum/gelatin in a large pan of very hot water and stirring the mixture until clear. Add to the cheese mixture. Beat the cream stiff and fold into the cheese.

Pour into 8 ceramic ramekins, top with 1 tsp. of guava jam, and chill for several hours—the jam may sink as the mousse chills. Just before serving, distribute a few slices of fresh guava on top, sprinkle liberally with sugar, and caramelize under the broiler or with a kitchen blowtorch.

Serves 8.

This may be found through the sources guide at the back of this book and is called goiabada cremosa.

Calda de Goiaba e Hortelã
Guava and Mint Soup

This soup should be served on a hot day, preferably in small, white bowls, cups, or sherbet glasses that allow the beautiful color to be seen.

1 lb. guava (about 3)
Water
10 mint leaves

Peel the guavas, cut in pieces, and beat smooth in the blender. Press through a sieve to remove the seeds. Measure the pulp and add an equal amount of water; stir well to combine. Wash the mint leaves, chop finely, and mix into the soup. Thin with a bit more water if necessary. Chill for several hours or overnight.

Serves 2-3.

Persimmon. The *caqui*, or persimmon, originated in China and arrived in Brazil in 1890 but only expanded its cultivation in the 1920s after immigration of the Japanese. Now Brazil is the second-largest producer of this fruit in the world, with persimmons principally grown in the state of São Paulo. Globally, there are many varieties of persimmon, but in this South American country, one finds three popular varieties. Two resemble large tomatoes and are bright orange both inside and out. The third, called a *chocolate caqui*, has a brown interior with large, oval, inedible seeds and dark fibers. Although the *chocolate caqui* is in great demand in Brazil, I personally find the brown color of the chocolate unattractive, and the seeds are always a hindrance in preparing the fruit for cooking.

Cheesecake com Caqui
Persimmon Cheesecake

Cheesecake arrived from America many years ago. As with other adoptions, Brazilians have put their own spin on the dessert, in this case, the addition of persimmon. Since graham crackers are unavailable in Brazil unless Americans bring them from the U.S., this recipe originally called for Maria Biscuit crumbs, a slightly sweet, dry cookie. I found that both graham crackers and cookie crumbs worked well.

Crust

2 cups graham cracker or cookie crumbs
½ cup butter or margarine
1 tsp. cinnamon
1 tsp. nutmeg
5 tbsp. confectioner's sugar

Filling

2 envelopes gelatin, unflavored
1 cup cold water
1 cup persimmon pulp, whipped briefly in the blender
8 oz. cream cheese
1 tsp. vanilla
1½ cups sugar
1 cup heavy cream

Crust

With a pastry blender, combine all ingredients for the crust. Butter a 9-inch spring-form pan or coat with non-stick spray. Turn the dough into the pan and, using the fingers, distribute evenly over the bottom, not the sides, of the pan. Press to obtain a firm, compact layer. Bake in a 350-degree oven for about 10 minutes or until it begins to brown slightly.

Filling

Combine the gelatin with water in a small bowl, let it rest for 5 minutes, and dissolve the mixture by setting the bowl in a pan of very hot water. Stir and remove from the hot water bath as soon as the gelatin has dissolved. Add persimmon pulp and mix together. Set aside.

With an electric mixer, beat cream cheese, vanilla, and sugar until light and airy and add the gelatin/persimmon mixture. In another bowl whip cream until stiff and carefully fold into the gelatin mixture. Turn the cheesecake into the cooked crust and refrigerate at least 2 hours or overnight.

Serves 10.

Caqui don Molho de Laranja com Sorvete
Persimmon in Orange Sauce with Ice Cream

Since you must peel and cut the persimmons into sections, use the firm

variety of persimmon for this dish. Originally, cinnamon ice cream was paired with the fruit, but cardamom or any other spicy ice cream works equally well. In a pinch, you can certainly use vanilla.

Juice of 4 oranges
1½ cups sugar
2 large persimmons
4 scoops of ice cream—cinnamon, cardamom, or other
Sprigs of mint
Poppy seeds

Mix the orange juice and sugar in a saucepan and, over a medium fire, cook for 7 minutes. Let the mixture cool. Peel the persimmons, cut each in 10 sections, and marinate them in the orange sauce for 1-3 hours. To serve, arrange 5 persimmon sections in a sunburst pattern on each plate, cover with sauce, and put an ice cream scoop in the center. Decorate with mint sprigs and sprinkle with poppy seeds.

Serves 4.

Star fruit, or *carambola,* are crisp and juicy, with a delicate flavor reminiscent of a combined apple and pear. Originating in India, this fruit was first introduced into Brazil in 1817 and is now grown in almost all parts of the country. Rich in vitamins A, C, and B complex, star fruit juice is used in Brazil to combat fever and diarrhea. When ripe, the fruit is yellow, firm, and totally edible, including the skin and seeds. Because it is so decorative, star fruit is cut crosswise into star-shaped slices and often appears as a garnish or as a part of fruit salads; star fruit pies, cakes, and sauces are also popular.

Bolo de Carambola
Star Fruit Upside-Down Cake

This is a first cousin to an American upside-down cake and quite beautiful with the decorative star fruit. If the edges of the fruit have turned a bit brown, trim them and cut in ¼- to ⅓-inch slices; be sure to remove all the seeds before fitting them into the pan.

2 cups sugar
½ cup water
6-8 ripe star fruit
4 eggs, separated
1 cup sugar
2 cups flour
1 scant tbsp. baking powder
1 cup star fruit juice*

In a saucepan, combine 2 cups of sugar and water. Bring to a boil, boil until the mixture turns caramel in color, and pour into a 9-inch pan with high sides or a 9-inch spring-form pan, making sure the syrup covers the bottom of the pan. Slice enough star fruit to cover the syrup and fit them into the liquid.

With the electric beater on high, beat the egg whites stiff and add the yolks while continuing to beat. Add the sugar and beat again. Combine the flour and baking powder and add to the batter alternately with the star fruit juice while beating on high speed. Pour over the star fruit in the pan and bake at 350 degrees F for approximately 1 hour 45 minutes or until the cake tests done. Remove from the oven and immediately invert on a plate.

Serves 10.

To make star fruit juice, combine 1 sliced star fruit, 1 cup to 1 ½ cups water, and the juice of ½ a lemon in the blender. Blend on high, then strain.

Other Popular Fruits

Citrus fruits were known to the Romans before the time of Christ and originated in Asia between India and the Himalayas at least two thousand years earlier. Brought to Brazil by the Portuguese, the **lime,** or *limão,* is used rather than the yellow lemon, which is difficult to grow in the tropics and, on the rare occasions it appears for sale in Brazil, extremely expensive. Of unknown origin, the full name of this hybrid fruit is *limão–taiti* because it was taken to California from Tahiti around 1875, and thence to Florida where it is still grown commercially. In Brazil, limes appear in an infinite number of dishes. Sometimes just a few drops of juice are used, or perhaps a grating of peel, and on other occasions, juice of the entire fruit. The *caipirinha,* Brazil's national cocktail, consists of whole, cut limes well mashed with sugar to which ice cubes and a generous amount of *cachaça* or fermented cane juice is added. The recipe may be found in the miscellaneous section of this book.

Popular in ancient Asia, the **orange,** or *laranja,* is one of the most cultivated fruits on the planet, with more than two thousand existing varieties. Brazil boasts only two, the *pêra* and the *lima.* The former is flavorful and sweet, a multipurpose orange used for juice, cooking, and eating, while the *lima,* with a much milder taste, is given to children, the elderly, and those suffering from digestive problems and hepatitis.

Large-scale commercial production of oranges in Brazil only commenced in the 1960s after an unprecedented frost destroyed a large part of the orange trees in Florida. As the biggest consumer of citrus juice in the world, the United States was forced to import this product, initiating the orange industry in Brazil. Today, oranges are grown in six Brazilian states, and the country is the largest exporter of orange juice in the world.

From Asia, *figos,* or **figs,** probably arrived in Brazil five hundred years ago, but before the twentieth century, they were only eaten raw and used in homemade compotes by those with fig trees in their gardens. Once picked, this fruit does not continue to ripen and, therefore, must be fully ripe when harvested. As a result, figs are fragile, difficult to handle and transport, and are sold almost exclusively in the markets of São Paulo state, close to the farms where they are grown. For protection, they are packed at the farms in small boxes containing eight figs.

Sugar apples, or **custard apples,** are known by a variety of names and are native to the Caribbean. In Brazil, they are called *fruta de Conde* or *pinha.* According to legend, in 1626 Conde de Miranda (Count Miranda) planted the first one in the state of Bahia. It took nearly two hundred years for the *pinha* to reach Rio de Janeiro, and only at the request of the emperor, Dom João II. Now cultivated throughout Brazil, they can be found all year round.

Pinha are always yellow-green with a knobby exterior that contains white, juicy flesh and inedible black seeds. A delicate fruit, *pinha* must be harvested when almost ripe and does not travel successfully. At the market, they are arranged in small, open boxes that must be hand-carried to prevent disintegration of the fruit. When mature, they are soft to the touch and should not be cut but pulled or broken into halves after which they are almost always eaten raw with a spoon.

Originating in Brazil and now grown throughout the tropical world, the *cajum,* or **cashew,** is a yellow fruit resembling a bell pepper in appearance.

When still green, it is used in the Brazilian northeast, in a shrimp dish to which Jorge Amado, Brazil's famous writer, referred to in his book *Tieta do Agreste*. The unfermented juice of the *caju* is rich in iron, magnesium, zinc, and copper and very popular; a delicious, fine wine is made from the fermented juice. In São Paulo, the fruit itself—which both my husband and myself find remarkably flavorless—is eaten raw or used in sweets such as ice cream, compotes, or is crystallized.

As a newcomer to Brazil, I was astonished to discover that the cashew nut, familiar to most Americans, grows within the fruit. These nuts, high in protein, are favorites of both adults and children and are sold from small stands at the feira, in paper cones at city intersections, and at all supermarkets.

There are at least a dozen varieties of **jabuticaba,** a fruit native to Brazil that is grown mainly in areas of thick vegetation. In appearance, these berries are similar to grapes, with smooth, tough dark skins, but they grow directly on the trunk and large branches of the tree. To eat them raw, one bites into the skin, squeezes the light-colored flesh and seeds into the mouth, and discards the skin, consuming both the pulp and soft seed. Obviously, it's not a fruit to serve at a dinner party.

Commercially, this fruit appears almost exclusively in jellies. Because the shelf life is short—four days maximum before the *jabuticaba* begin to ferment—the fresh berries appear only sporadically, principally in feiras rather than supermarkets. When grown in backyard gardens, the domestic chef uses sugar syrup from cooked berries in desserts or as an accompaniment to meat or chicken.

Originally from Asia, *amora,* or **mulberries,** are now grown throughout Brazil. Rich in vitamin C, this fruit is eaten raw and used in jellies as well as transformed into wines and liqueurs. *Amora* grows on trees planted in all areas of São Paulo. In mulberry season, one often sees clusters of children and adults gathered under the trees in public parks, picking and eating the berries. For some unknown reason, this easily grown, common fruit never appears at the feira or on restaurant menus and can only be purchased in upscale boutique markets at high prices.

4

Chicken and Other Fowl

A pleasant, easy-going man in his forties, Sinésio took over ownership of this family-run feira business several years ago, and his management style is clearly apparent. Unlike the rough and tumble atmosphere prevalent in some of the stands, quiet, good manners, and pleasant service is the rule here. One of the few stands in the feira with employees wearing immaculate uniforms and hair tucked into caps, Sinésio's employees are not only polite and efficient, but have clearly been trained to maintain high hygienic standards. During the day, the bulk of the poultry is stored within the firm's white, refrigerated truck parked just behind the stand on the sidewalk. On weekdays, Sinésio takes telephone orders and, regardless of the amount requested, his employees deliver throughout the city.

When Sinésio's sister sees us approaching, she fills two tiny paper cups with heavily sweetened, super-strong coffee from a gigantic thermos and offers them to us on a small, plastic tray. We chat about our families, the weather, the upcoming holiday—anything and everything—while we drink the hot, typically Brazilian coffee that fortifies the employees throughout

the morning. Only after dropping the empty cups in the trash and thanking Sinésio's sister effusively do we get down to business and discuss chickens.

Although cut legs, breasts, and thighs are carefully displayed and recognizable, a whole chicken, cut-up, is another matter. After the customer selects a fowl, it is taken to a butcher block where the machete flies, whacking the unfortunate bird into at least twelve pieces, all but legs and wings unidentifiable, and seemingly chopped according to size rather than carved into body parts. The finished package will also contain heads, necks, feet, livers, and gizzards, but a heart will never be included. Available by the kilo and in great demand for Brazilian barbeques, chicken hearts are sold separately at the far end of the counter.

When requested, chickens will be deboned, packaged according to directions, and even marinated. If ordered ahead, Sinésio will bring a rabbit, turkey, or duck, cut and prepared as specifically instructed.

Canja
Chicken Soup

This traditional, classic Brazilian chicken soup is served all over Brazil. Needless to say, there are endless variations. While many of them include sausage, some have clear broth, and others are thick; rice is a mandatory ingredient in all. *Canja* is not served as a first course but always as a main dish, usually accompanied by Italian bread.

2 tbsp. salad oil
2 small onions, finely chopped
1 large clove garlic, minced
½ tsp. grated ginger
2 chicken breasts
½ cup rice, uncooked
1 medium carrot, chopped
1 medium potato, cubed
1 ½ qt. chicken stock
2 sprigs basil
Salt and pepper, to taste
¼ cup parsley, chopped
1 green onion, thinly sliced

Fry onions in oil in a large saucepan. Add garlic and ginger, frying for 2 minutes more, and add chicken breasts, browning lightly. Add rice and stir to coat grains with oil. Add carrot, potato, stock, basil, and salt and pepper; cover; and simmer until vegetables and chicken are thoroughly cooked. When cooled a bit, take out chicken breasts, debone, and cube the meat. Return to soup along with parsley and green onion, adding more stock if necessary. Reheat when ready to serve.

Serves 5.

Salpicão de Frango e Palmito
Chicken Salad with Hearts of Palm

If smoked chicken isn't available, ordinary chicken is perfectly fine in this light and delicious luncheon dish.

2 cups shredded smoked chicken breast
1 cup chopped onion
1 cup julienned apple
½ cup light raisins
½ cup sliced hearts of palm
½ cup grated carrot
½ cup parsley, chopped
½ cup each julienned red and green pepper
½ cup julienned celery
2 cups mayonnaise
2 tbsp. Worcestershire sauce

2 tbsp. mustard
Salt and pepper, to taste
Lettuce
¼ cup chopped Brazil nuts or cashews

Combine the chicken, onion, apple, raisins, hearts of palm, carrot, parsley, peppers, and celery together. Blend the mayonnaise, Worcestershire, mustard, salt, and pepper and add to the chicken mixture. Line a platter with an assortment of lettuce leaves, mound the chicken salad in the center, and scatter nuts on top.

Serves 6.

Torta de Frango
Chicken Pie

Paulistanos are fond of main-dish pies of all kinds, and this is a good way to use leftover chicken. This is a basic filling to which you might add a few cooked mushrooms, a small chili pepper, frozen peas, or whatever you fancy.

Dough
2 cups flour
1 tsp. salt
⅓ cup vegetable oil
⅓ cup butter or margarine
A few tbsp. ice water

Filling
1 tbsp. butter or margarine
1 medium onion, chopped
2 cloves garlic, minced
3 cups cooked chicken, shredded
2 tomatoes, chopped
¼ cup green olives, chopped
½ cup chopped red or green pepper
2 tsp. chopped fresh rosemary
¼ cup water
2 tbsp. flour
Salt and pepper, to taste
2 tbsp. each chopped parsley and green onion

Dough

Sift the flour and salt into a bowl. Add the oil and butter and mix with fingers or a pastry blender until mixture crumbles. Add the water slowly, using only enough to hold the dough together and mixing only to bind. Cover and leave in refrigerator for 30 minutes.

Filling

Heat butter or margarine in a large pan and fry the onion and garlic until the onion is transparent. Add the chicken, tomatoes, green olives, peppers, and rosemary and cook for 5 minutes. Mix flour with the ¼ cup water until the flour has dissolved, pour onto the chicken mixture in the pan, and stir over low heat until it thickens. Take off the burner and add salt and pepper to taste along with the parsley and green onion. Let filling cool.

To Serve

Divide the dough in half, one slightly larger than the other. Roll out the bigger half between two sheets of plastic film or wax paper to a disk of 13 inches. Use this to line a 10-inch pie pan and fill the dough-lined pan with cooled chicken filling. Roll out the remaining dough into a disk to cover the pie, arrange on top of the chicken mixture, and pinch all around the edges to seal the dough.

Bake at 350 degrees F for 40 minutes or until the pie is golden and the crust flaky.

Serves 6-8.

Capote com Arroz
Guinea Fowl with Rice

I suspect, although I don't really know, that this is a recipe from the days when guinea fowl were more plentiful than chickens. That isn't the case any longer, and although the recipe has retained its original name, I found it superb when made with chicken thighs and legs. Turmeric and saffron come from India and were brought to Brazil by the Portuguese. Because saffron was so much more expensive and harder to obtain than turmeric, the latter spice gradually gained importance in the kitchen.

1 guinea fowl, or 8 chicken thighs
4 cloves garlic, chopped
½ tsp. salt
1 tsp. vinegar
½ tsp. cumin powder
2 tsp. turmeric
3 tbsp. vegetable oil
1 large onion, chopped
3 tomatoes, seeded and chopped
1 cup rice
4 cups chicken broth
Salt, to taste
1 small, hot pepper, finely minced
½ cup cilantro leaves, chopped

If using a guinea fowl, cut it in pieces. Season either guinea fowl or chicken with garlic, salt, vinegar, cumin, and turmeric. Heat the oil and brown the chicken until all liquid evaporates. Add onion and tomatoes and cook over a low flame, adding hot water as needed so the mixture doesn't dry out or burn. When the chicken tests done, add the rice, the chicken broth, and more salt if needed and simmer until the rice is al dente—about 20 minutes. To serve, turn the rice onto a platter, surround with chicken, and sprinkle with hot pepper and chopped cilantro.

Serves 6.

Frango Xinxim
Chicken and Shrimp Stew

Chicken *Xinxim* exists in dozens of variations, and it is very forgiving. Add or subtract ingredients if you like; it will still have authentic Brazilian flavor. *Dendê* (palm oil) can be found in some specialty shops (see sources guide), but it can be omitted altogether if necessary. In the northern state of Bahia, this oil is used exclusively, but it is very high in cholesterol. When I use it, which is rare, I add only a spoonful or two for flavor. Dried shrimp can be found in Asian shops and lend a distinctive taste that cannot otherwise be duplicated.

Chicken and Other Fowl

1 medium chicken, cut into serving pieces
Salt and pepper
Juice of 2 limes
2 tbsp. vegetable oil
1 lb. shrimp, peeled
2 tbsp. olive oil
1 onion, chopped
2 cloves garlic, minced
2 tbsp. roasted peanuts
2 tbsp. roasted cashews
½ cup dried shrimp, rinsed
2 tomatoes, peeled and chopped
1 cup chicken stock, preferably homemade
1 hot chili pepper, minced
1 tbsp. *dendê* oil, light
½ cup fresh cilantro, chopped
½ cup unsweetened coconut milk
Salt, to taste

Season the chicken with salt and pepper and marinate in the juice of 1 lime for 30 minutes. Heat 2 tbsp. vegetable oil in a large skillet and sauté the shrimp until pink. Remove and reserve. Add olive oil to the same pan and sauté the chicken in batches, browning well and adding more oil if needed. Remove. In the same pan, sauté the onion and garlic until translucent. Grind the roasted peanuts, cashews, dried shrimp, and tomatoes together and add to the onion mixture. Return the chicken to the pan, add the chicken stock and minced chili pepper, cover, and cook for about 40 minutes or until the chicken is done, stirring occasionally.

When done, add the shrimp along with the *dendê* and cilantro and simmer for 10 minutes. Pour in the coconut milk and the juice of the remaining lime. Taste for salt. Serve with white rice.

Serves 4.

Frango Assado Com Alho
Roast Chicken with Garlic

Because the chicken is semihalved and flattened, it takes less time to roast than the conventional method, browns well, is easier to test done, and is just

as successful if only half is roasted. At first glance, the amount of garlic seems overwhelming, but the cloves only lend a subtle flavor to the meat.

1 medium chicken, cut through the back bone and flattened
1 tsp. salt
2 tsp. garlic grains or powder
1 tbsp. chopped parsley
Pepper, to taste
2 tbsp. mustard
2 tbsp. Worcestershire sauce
2 tsp. dried oregano
3 large onions
2 heads garlic

Wash the chicken, inside and out, and dry. Mix the next 7 ingredients and rub onto the chicken, both inside and out, including under the skin. Place the chicken in a glass bowl, cover tightly (or place in a plastic bag and close securely), and allow to rest in the refrigerator for a minimum of 2 hours. Meanwhile, peel and slice the onions and scatter in a roasting pan that has been greased with olive

oil. Wash the garlic but do not peel and cut each clove in half. After marinating, place the chicken, skin side up, on the bed of onions and press the garlic cloves, cut side down, onto the chicken. Roast at 350 degrees in a medium oven for 1½ hours or until it tests done. Turn off the oven and allow to rest for 5-10 minutes, and then discard the garlic. Cut into quarters.

Serves 4.

Galinha de Tia Maria Rosa
Aunt Mary Rose's Chicken

Cachaça is alcohol made in Brazil from sugar cane and is available in large liquor shops in the U.S. If absolutely necessary, cognac or light rum could be substituted, but it does change the flavor of the dish. Before the 1960s, mushrooms were not included in Brazilian cuisine. Sometime during that decade, the agaricus mushroom was discovered in the state of São Paulo by researcher and grower Takatoshi Furumoto who cultivated it for a few years. After his death, farming of the fungus died out but was revived in the 1990s; as a result, the cuisine of São Paulo today frequently includes mushrooms.

1 whole chicken, cut up
2 onions, sliced
Butter

¼ cup *cachaça*
3 tomatoes, chopped
1 mildly hot chili pepper, chopped
½ lb. mushrooms, sliced
Salt, to taste
3 hard-boiled eggs

Sauté the chicken and onions in butter. Add the cachaça or cognac, tomatoes, and pepper; cover; and cook over low heat. Meanwhile, sauté the mushrooms and chop the eggs. When the chicken is done, add the mushrooms, taste for salt, turn into a serving dish, and sprinkle with chopped egg.

Serves 6-8.

Frango Caipira
Hillbilly Chicken

A few years ago, my husband and I were traveling through Piauí, one of the poorest and most economically backward states, and stopped for the night in a small town with one tiny restaurant boasting two wooden tables in a room open to the street and sky. There was no menu, but the bent and aging proprietor told us they were serving Frango Caipira, prepared by his wife in the minute galley kitchen a few feet away. That tasty dish was accompanied by rice, beans, and potatoes and was just one of hundreds of variations of this culinary concoction served throughout Brazil—all of them subject to interpretation by the cook. This particular version is distinguished by the addition of chicken hearts and liver, but its success depends on the chicken stock. Because broth is easy to make (see miscellaneous chapter) and the flavor is so superior to cubes or canned stock, it is worth keeping a quart or two in the freezer for handy use.

8 chicken hearts
2-3 chicken livers
1 medium chicken, cut up
4 tbsp. vegetable oil
1 onion
2 large cloves garlic
½ cup dry white wine
1 qt. chicken stock
1½ cups rice
Salt

Remove all fat from the hearts, cut in half, and wash under running water. Clean the livers well, cut in 4 pieces, and wash under running water. Wash the chicken in water and dry. Chop the onion and garlic.

Heat 1 tbsp. of oil in a large pot, add the hearts and livers, and sauté rapidly. Remove and reserve them. In the same pot, sauté the pieces of chicken, adding more oil if necessary and remove from pan when browned. Sauté the onion and garlic in the same pan until soft but not brown, scraping the bottom of the pan to loosen the browned bits, which carry a lot of flavor. Return the chicken pieces—but not the hearts and livers—to the pot, pour in the wine, and evaporate over a moderate fire (about 5 minutes). Add the stock, lower the heat, and cook for 30 minutes, covering the pan halfway through.

Add the hearts and livers and stir in the rice. Cover the pot again and cook for about 20 minutes or until the rice is done. Check halfway through to make sure there is sufficient broth. When done, adjust the salt if necessary.

Serves 6.

Arroz de Forno
Oven Rice

This is a delicious recipe that can be made during the day and slipped into the oven about thirty minutes before serving. It is also a great way to use leftover rice.

1 medium chicken, cut in pieces
3 tbsp. oil
7 oz. chicken livers
1 onion, chopped
2 cloves garlic, minced
4 tomatoes, chopped
Salt, to taste
1 hot chili pepper, chopped
½ cup water
2 cups raw rice, cooked
10 oz. package frozen peas
4 eggs, hard-boiled and sliced
½ lb. mozzarella, sliced
1 cup grated Parmesan

Brown the chicken in oil. Add the chicken livers, onion, and garlic and cook until the onion is soft. Add the tomatoes, salt, chili pepper, and water and cook, covered, until the chicken is done. Remove the chicken and debone. Combine the deboned chicken and liver mixture with the cooked rice and add the peas. Butter a large casserole and spread it with half the rice mixture. Distribute the sliced egg and mozzarella over the surface and top with the rest of the rice. Sprinkle with Parmesan and bake at 400 degrees for 10 or 15 minutes or until the cheese starts to brown.

Serves 8-10.

Confit de Pato com Purê de Batatas
Preserved Duck and Potato Purée

I first tasted this delicious duck dish at Confraria, a chic restaurant in Campos do Jordão, a fashionable resort in the São Paulo mountains. Creator of the dish, Chef Fernando Ricardo Couto and his wife and restaurant co-owner, Cristina, graciously agreed to share the recipe with me.

Chicken and Other Fowl

Confit

4 duck quarters (leg and thigh), weighing about 12 oz. each
4 green apples, peeled and grated
4 branches thyme
Salt and pepper

Black Cherry Sauce

4 tbsp. black cherry jam
Cooled stock made from cooked duck
Salt and pepper, to taste

Purée of Potatoes

1½ lb. potatoes
½ cup butter
1 cup cream
Salt and pepper, to taste
½ cup Serra da Estrela cheese*

Confit

Put 1 duck quarter, 1 grated apple, the leaves of 1 branch of thyme, and salt and pepper in each of 4 Ziploc-type bags big enough to accommodate with extra room. Close the bags and place in a large pan of simmering water, making sure that the zip fastener is on top and out of the water. Cook for approximately 7 hours or until the meat is soft, checking from time to time to add more water and confirm that the fasteners are above water level. When done, remove the bags from the water, carefully pour the liquid, which is now stock, into a large bowl, reserve the duck quarters in another container, and allow both to cool. When the stock is quite cold, chill in the refrigerator, remove the fat, and put the rest through the blender. Reserve.

Black Cherry Sauce

Combine the jam and stock in a small pan and cook to reduce somewhat. Adjust the salt and pepper.

Purée of Potatoes

Cook the potatoes, peel them, and mash. Combine all the ingredients, mix well, and serve hot.

To Serve

Heat the duck in its sauce in a 200-degree oven, then brown the duck, skin side up, under the grill. Pile the puréed potatoes in the center of a platter, top with the duck, and distribute the sauce over all.

Serves 4.

Serra da Estrela cheese is the king of Portuguese cheese, handmade from ewe's milk in the highest and coldest mountains of Portugal. It is very soft, occasionally can be found in specialty cheese or grocery shops, and, when available, is extremely expensive in Brazil. If it is not possible to use this specific cheese, substitute soft sheep's or goat's cheese; the flavor will be different but still delectable.

5

Vegetables

This stand is twice as long as others at the feira and, for the most part, displays produce found all over America, including carrots, cauliflower, beets, okra, bell peppers of all colors and sizes, cucumbers, and at least eight varieties of lettuce. Although one can find a few curious culinary botanical growths here that usually are not much appreciated by the non-Brazilian, the primary differences between the vegetables of this country and those of the United States are cultural. For example, peas are usually sold shelled, beets are frequently precooked, and winter squash is often sold in slices or peeled and cubed. Broccoli rabe is known as common broccoli and much cheaper than the broccoli rabe sold in North America, but it is very tough and must be stewed for a long time. Though there are exceptions, vegetables are generally used as ingredients in main or accompanying dishes rather than appearing as, for instance, as a side dish of string beans or beets.

Luiz is proprietor of our preferred vegetable stand. Unlike other owners, he spends his time supervising his many employees rather than serving customers. Seemingly everywhere, he strides the length of his vegetable domain adjusting the slant of the canvas shade, changing prices, replenishing dwindling displays, and, above all, keeping a sharp eye on the money. Although Luiz's stand includes lettuce and related greens such as arugula, radicchio, leeks, and watercress, Ezio, one of our feira favorites, independently runs this particular section. A retired banker, we have never seen him without his battered straw hat; long, denim apron; and green

rubber gloves, nor have we ever known him to continue sorting lettuce when we appear. Although he has failed to mention any other family members, we receive weekly updates about his daughter, of whom he is inordinately proud. A human resources director for an international pharmaceutical company, she speaks several languages fluently, flies throughout the world on business, and has just bought a house in one of São Paulo's most prestigious sections. We know her birthday, where and when she vacations, and all about her taste in furnishings—just about everything but her name. Before asking Ezio to choose the best heads of lettuce, we slide into a rousing discussion concerning politicians and the latest Brazilian political scandal, subjects guaranteed to bring hoots of laughter to all. The bells of Nossa Senhora da Consolação remind me that it's time to make a serious selection of vegetables.

Crème de Abóbora com Camarão
Cream of Squash Soup with Shrimp

Use any winter squash but spaghetti squash in this soup. The flavor of the finished product is substantially improved if you make your own stock, which is quite simple if you have access to a fishmonger or a supermarket where fish are cleaned and scaled. Ask for about a pound of bones, including the head, or use shrimp shells. Wash and toss into a large kettle. Add an onion, celery stalk, and a few parsley sprigs, all chopped, as well as some peppercorns, a teaspoon or two of salt, a small bay leaf, one cup of dry white wine, and two quarts of water. Bring to a boil and barely simmer, uncovered, for about fifty minutes. Strain it and use in this recipe; then freeze any leftover stock for future use in sauces or other fish soups.

3 lb. squash, peeled and cut up
3 cups fish stock, approximately
1 medium onion, chopped
2 cloves garlic, minced
1 hot chili pepper, minced
Vegetable oil
1-inch ginger, grated
¾ cup coconut milk (light, if available)
1 lb. medium shrimp, peeled and cleaned
Salt, to taste

Vegetables

Cook the squash in a minimum of water. When it is soft, put it through the blender, using enough stock to liquefy. The amounts of both water and stock will vary according to the type of squash used, but don't thin it too much at this point. Sweat the onion, garlic, and chili pepper in a little oil and, when softened, add the squash mixture and the ginger. Cook for 5 or 10 minutes and add the coconut milk. Meanwhile, sauté the shrimp in oil. When pink, add the shrimp to the soup. Adjust the salt and, if necessary, thin with more stock.

Serves 6.

Caldinho de Abóbora
Squash Soup

Dulce Muniz has based this creation on her recipe for bean soup.

2 lb. winter squash (any variety but spaghetti), cooked
4 cups water (more or less)
2 medium onions, chopped
1 tbsp. minced ginger
1 cup loosely packed fresh cilantro leaves
1 fresh red pepper, seeded
3 tbsp. olive oil
2 cloves garlic, minced
Salt and pepper, to taste

In the blender, beat the squash with increasing amounts of water until the soup is almost smooth and slightly thinner than the finished product. Add the onions, ginger, cilantro, and red pepper; blend again and reserve. Pour olive oil into a cooking pot and sauté the garlic, cooking only until it is very light tan, as it will turn bitter with browning. Add the contents of the blender, salt and pepper, and cook on low heat for 20 minutes or until it has amalgamated and thickened, stirring from time to time. Add salt and pepper and take from the fire.

Accompany the soup with the following, each in a small dish to be passed around the table.

1. 4-6 large cloves garlic, minced and sautéed
2. Fresh ginger, grated
3. Cilantro leaves, finely chopped
4. 6 fresh red peppers, seeded and minced

Serves 6.

Sopa de Abóbora com Hortelã
Squash Soup with Mint

With very few ingredients, this unusual and delicious soup is easy and quick to make. It can be whipped up for an informal family meal or confidently served at a dinner party.

2 lb. winter squash (any variety but spaghetti), peeled and cut into cubes
1 large onion, chopped
4 cups beef stock, homemade, from a cube, or canned
1 cup mint leaves, chopped
Salt and pepper
Sour cream

In a large pot, cook the squash, onion, and meat stock for 20 minutes or until the squash is soft, stirring from time to time. Pour soup into a blender, add mint, and beat until smooth, with flecks of green mint. Taste for salt and pepper and serve very hot with a dollop of sour cream topping each soup bowl.
Serves 8.

Quibebe
Quibebe

This dish frequently appears as both an accompaniment to meat, chicken, and fish and also as the main plate at a luncheon, together with a salad and bread. As in many traditional Brazilian dishes, the ingredients are variable; vegetarians can omit the bacon and the finished product will still be an authentic *quibebe*.

3 thick slices bacon, cubed
1 tbsp. olive oil
3 cloves garlic, chopped
4 onions, chopped
Pinch of sugar
2 lb. winter squash (any variety), in ¾-inch cubes
Salt and pepper, to taste
Water
6-8 scallions, chopped
½ cup parsley, chopped

In a large pot, sauté the bacon cubes until they begin to brown. Pour off the fat and add the olive oil, garlic, and onions. When the onions and garlic are transparent, add the sugar, squash, salt and pepper to taste, and about an inch of water. Cover and cook over low heat, stirring carefully from time to time and adding additional water if necessary. Cooking time will depend on the type of squash and the size of the pieces, but it will take approximately 20-30 minutes. When done, taste for seasoning, mash to a purée, turn into a serving dish, and top with the chopped scallions and parsley.

Serves 6.

Salada de Tomates e Búfalo com Pesto da Pimenta
Mozzarella and Tomato Salad with Chili Pesto

Fresh mozzarella—called *búfalo*—is made from buffalo milk, and the largest number of water buffalo can be found on Ilha de Marajó. In fact, there are more buffalo than humans on this piece of land and a fair number of the animals are wild. Local lore claims that water buffalo arrived on Marajó, located on the Equator at the mouth of the Amazon River, due to a shipwreck in the nineteenth century. As passengers on this unfortunate vessel, the animals presumably swam to shore where they have remained and multiplied ever since. At any rate, they have a great deal of space in which to roam, as this is the largest island in the world that is completely surrounded by fresh water.

2 or more chili peppers, minced
6 black olives
2 tbsp. chopped parsley
2 tbsp. olive oil
Salt, to taste
4 tomatoes, sliced
3 large balls of mozzarella, sliced
Watercress
Arugula leaves

Combine all ingredients except tomatoes, mozzarella, arugula, and watercress. On a serving platter, arrange alternate slices of tomatoes and cheese and loop a thread of pesto over all. Surround with watercress or arugula leaves.

Serves 4.

Tomates Cereja Assado
Oven-Baked Cherry Tomatoes

Although widely used in any number of ways, there is little variety in the kinds of tomatoes found in Brazil. They are always red, medium size, and plum shaped or round. Cherry tomatoes are expensive, considered fairly exotic, and can only be found in feiras and upscale markets.

2 tsp. grated lemon rind
1 clove garlic, minced
2 tbsp. olive oil
½ cup breadcrumbs
1 lb. cherry tomatoes
3 tbsp. fresh basil or parsley, chopped
½ tsp. salt

Heat oven to 450 degrees F. In a small skillet, cook the lemon rind and garlic in l tbsp. olive oil until the garlic begins to color. Add crumbs and fry until toasted. Reserve. Grease an ovenproof dish just large enough to hold the tomatoes in one layer. Roll tomatoes in oil in pan and bake tomatoes for 10 minutes or until the skin begins to break. Mix the basil and salt with the breadcrumb mixture and sprinkle over the tomatoes.

Serves 4.

Chu-chu com Presunto e Mussarelas
Chayote with Ham and Mozzarella

Brazilians love *chu-chu* (pronounced shoo-shoo and often spelled *xu-xu*), or chayote, in any form, including steamed with a sprinkling of olive oil and salt. Like most Americans, I think this vegetable is far too bland to be served unadorned but is a wonderful accompaniment to meat, fish, or chicken when combined with other, more strongly flavored ingredients. This very versatile dish may serve as the first course for dinner, a side dish, or the main plate for lunch. In the latter case, the amount of cheese and ham must be increased and each person should be presented with two halves.

2 medium chayote, halved
4 oz. ham
4 oz. mozzarella
Curry paste, to taste
Salt, to taste
Parsley sprigs

Steam the chayote until tender and scoop out the flesh, being careful to leave an unbroken shell. (I have found a melon scoop works well for this task.) Discard the seed and chop the chayote flesh, shred the ham or cut in small cubes, and shred the mozzarella. Mix, add salt to taste, and pile back into the chayote shells. Bake in a 350-degree oven for 15 minutes. Garnish with parsley sprigs and serve immediately.

Serves 2 for lunch or 4 as a first course.

Suflê De Chu-Chu
Chayote Soufflé

This impressive dish, a perfect companion for any chicken or meat, has been popular in São Paulo for many years. Much easier to put together than the average soufflé, it is frequently served instead of potatoes or another mild vegetable. Like any soufflé, it must be eaten immediately after removal from the oven.

1 lb. chayote, diced
6 large eggs, separated
3 tbsp. flour
½ tsp. salt, or to taste
½ cup milk
3 tbsp. Parmesan

Peel chayotes, cut in half, and remove the seeds. Boil or steam the halves until very tender and then dice finely. Beat the egg yolks. Sift the flour and salt together. To the eggs, add the chayote, sifted flour and salt, milk, and Parmesan. Beat the egg whites until stiff, fold into chayote mixture, and pour into a greased soufflé dish. Bake at 350 degrees for 30-40 minutes or until top is golden.

Serves 4.

Sopa Fria de Chuchu e Capim-santo
Cold Chayote Soup with Lemongrass

This beautiful, delicately flavored soup is the creation of Chef Quentin Geenen de Saint Maur and appears in his book *Muito Prazer, Brasil*. When served in soup plates and garnished with edible flowers, it is spectacular.

2 tbsp. grated fresh ginger
1 qt. chicken stock
3 medium chayote, peeled, seeded, and cubed
1 tbsp. vegetable oil
5 or 6 lemongrass stalks, crushed and chopped
Salt and pepper, to taste

Mix the ginger into the chicken stock and bring to a boil. Turn down the fire and simmer, covered, while the chayote cubes are briefly sautéed in oil until slightly softened. Combine the chayote and chicken stock and simmer until the chayote is cooked. Turn off the fire, add the lemongrass, and cool to room temperature. Strain, pressing on the pulp so that only the lemongrass shreds remain in the sieve. Adjust the seasoning and chill for several hours. Garnish with edible flowers.

Serves 4.

Salada de Chu-Chu
Chayote Slaw

This light salad can precede any type of meal. If you prefer less spicy food, eliminate the chili pepper and use less spice mix. The spice mix keeps very well if tightly capped in a cool place and can also be rubbed on fish before grilling or sautéing.

1 tbsp. oil
4 cups chayote, cut in matchsticks (more or less 2 medium chayotes)
1 red bell pepper, roasted and cut in matchsticks
1 yellow bell pepper, roasted and cut in matchsticks
1 hot chili pepper, minced
⅓ cup sherry vinegar
2 tsp. Brazil spice mix (see miscellaneous)
½ cup olive oil
2 tsp. chopped fresh cilantro

Heat oil in a skillet and sauté the chayote until tender-crisp, about 8 minutes. Cool and combine with the bell peppers and chili pepper. In a bowl, blend the vinegar, spice mix, oil, and cilantro, then combine with the chayote and mix well.

Serves 4-5.

Chu-Chu Ao Forno
Chayote in the Oven

This recipe demonstrates the adaptability of chayote squash when combined with more robust flavors. The joy of this dish is that it may be prepared early in the day and slipped into the oven just before serving. For an authentic flavor, manioc meal should be used, but if it isn't available, cornmeal or fine, dry breadcrumbs may be substituted.

1 chayote
1 onion, chopped
2 tomatoes, peeled and seeded
2 tbsp. olive oil
½ cup light coconut milk
Cilantro, chopped
1 tsp. salt, or to taste
1 tbsp. grated Parmesan
1 tbsp. manioc meal

Peel and coarsely grate the chayote, discarding the seed. Sauté the onion, chayote, and tomatoes in oil for 10 minutes. Add the coconut milk, cilantro, and salt. Mix in the Parmesan and pour into an oven-proof dish. Sprinkle the top with manioc meal and heat in a hot oven for 10 minutes just before serving.

Serves 3-4.

Caldo Verde
Green Soup

The easiest way to shred kale leaves is to remove the central stalk, stack, roll tightly into a bundle, and slice them into thin ribbons. This hearty soup doesn't keep well as leftovers; although the flavor is unchanged, the leaves swell and the soup thickens. This soup is often served as a light supper on cold nights, accompanied by wine and Pão de Queijo (see index).

6 oz. kale leaves, cut in fine ribbons
2 lb. potatoes
8 oz. spicy sausage, whole
2 large cloves garlic, minced
1 large onion, chopped
2 qt. water
3 strips bacon, chopped
Salt
6 tsp. olive oil

Wash the kale leaves, cut off stalks, and remove the inner rib. Stack one on top of the other, roll up tightly, and slice in fine strips with a sharp knife. Peel the potatoes and cut in large pieces. Put potatoes in a pan with sausage, garlic, onion, and 2 qt. water. Boil lightly until the potatoes are soft. Remove the sausage and reserve. Cool the soup, whirl in the blender until nearly smooth, and return to the pan. Sauté the bacon until crisp. Add the bacon and kale to the soup and cook for about 10 minutes. Season with salt. Slice the cooked sausage and add to soup. Drizzle individual servings with olive oil.

Serves 8.

Couve à Mineira
Kale from Minas Gerais

Brazilians love this strong, green vegetable prepared very simply. The dish frequently appears on buffet tables or as an accompaniment to meat, especially pork, and is perfectly paired with Tutu de Feijão and Feijão Tropeiro (see index). In the feira, a rudimentary machine slices the leaves into matchstick-thin ribbons, but the home cook can duplicate this by shredding as explained in the recipe.

1 lb. kale
1 slice bacon, or 1 tbsp. olive oil
Salt, to taste

Wash the kale, cut off stalks, and remove the inner rib. Stack one on top of the other, roll up tightly, and slice in fine strips with a sharp knife. Scald in boiling water and drain well. Cut the bacon in small dice and fry in a skillet, or if you use olive oil, add it to the skillet. Fry the kale over high heat for 5 minutes, stirring constantly, and add salt to taste.

Serves 4.

Pimentões Coloridos
Colored Bell Pepper Hors d'oeuvre

This is an unusual change from the heavier pâtés often served with cocktails and is yet another way Brazilians use ricotta. Accompany these slices with small, square toasts.

3 red bell peppers
3 yellow bell peppers
1 envelope gelatin
2 tbsp. water
2 cups ricotta cheese
½ cup mayonnaise
2 tbsp. minced mint leaves
Salt and pepper, to taste

Wash the peppers and roast them, either directly over a gas flame, turning as they blacken, or in a hot oven. When roasted, let them rest for at least 15 minutes in a plastic bag, then carefully slip off the skins. Try not to do this under water as it somewhat dilutes the flavor. Cut them in half, remove the seeds and stems, place each one on a piece of plastic film, and reserve.

In a small bowl, soak the gelatin in water for 5 minutes, then dissolve over hot water or in a hot water bath. Beat the ricotta with the mayonnaise, mint, salt, and pepper until all is well blended, then beat in the liquid gelatin. Dry

the peppers well, divide the mixture among the 12 pepper halves, and, with the help of the plastic film, roll up to form cylinders. Chill in the refrigerator for at least 3 hours or until firm. To serve, cut in ½-inch slices, arrange on a platter, and decorate with mint sprigs.

Serves 8-10.

Marinada de Abobrinha e Pimenta
Marinated Zucchini Salad

Brazilians particularly love zucchini, possibly due to the influence of Italian immigrants to the south. Once I even found baby zucchini with the flowers still attached in the feira and was able to experiment with one stuffing for the flower and another for the vegetable, which was scrumptious but took most of the day and was far too labor intensive to repeat. Oddly enough, the yellow zucchini has never made it to Brazil, nor has the crookneck or patty-pan, all of which are summer squash and would be perfect in this mild to hot climate. This particular recipe may be successfully expanded to serve any

Vegetables

number of guests, either as a first course or as part of a buffet or potluck. Just remember that it absolutely must marinate for at least two hours.

1 large zucchini
1 clove garlic, crushed or minced
1 tbsp. sugar
½ tsp. salt
2 tbsp. white wine vinegar
1 hot chili pepper, minced
1 tbsp. oil
1 large spray of dill
1 tbsp. basil, finely chopped
1 tbsp. toasted sesame seeds

Slice the zucchini ⅛ inch thick (I get better results with less frustration when a slicer is used). Crush or mince the garlic and mix in the sugar, salt, and wine vinegar, stirring to dissolve. Combine with the rest of the ingredients, except the zucchini and sesame seeds, and mix well. Add the zucchini and turn into a container that allows the squash to bathe, at least partially, in the liquid. Marinate in the refrigerator at least 2 hours or overnight, turning over occasionally with a wooden spoon. Arrange on individual plates or on a platter and sprinkle with sesame seeds.

Serves 3.

Bolo de Milho Verde
Sweet Corn Cake

Corn, in its many forms, is extremely popular in Brazil; kernels appear in tossed and composed salads, polenta is offered in elegant as well as simple restaurants, and carts similar to those selling hot dogs are seen in parks and on street corners where the vendors steam ears of corn and hand them, buttered in a paper napkin, to clients. There are also many sweet dishes featuring corn as the principal ingredient, including corn ice cream and dried white hominy cooked as a pudding in milk, sugar, and cinnamon that are, to a North American palate, quite odd. This large cake is slightly sweet, with a faint flavor of cornbread but with a much finer texture. This could be served at breakfast, brunch, a buffet, or as an after-school snack. I've taken it to potlucks, where it is always applauded as delicious and different.

2½ cups drained, canned corn
½ cup milk
4 large eggs
3 ½ tbsp. butter, melted and cooled
2 ½ cups flour
1 ½ cups sugar
1 tsp. salt
1 tbsp. baking powder
Cinnamon and sugar to sprinkle on top

Preheat oven to 350 degrees F. Pulse the corn and milk in the processor or blender until thick and the kernels are crushed. Add the eggs and butter and blend until as smooth as possible. Thoroughly mix the flour, sugar, salt, and baking powder in a bowl, then combine with the corn mixture, blending well with a wooden spoon.

Grease and flour a 9-inch spring-form pan, pour in the cake batter, and bake for 1 hour and 15 minutes or until it tests done. When done, the cake will be golden brown on top and small crumbs will cling to the toothpick tester. Remove from the pan and cool on a rack. While warm, sprinkle the top with about ½ cup sugar combined with ground cinnamon to taste.

Serves 12.

Caldo de Cenoura with Tomilho e Iogurte
Carrot Soup with Thyme and Yogurt

The flavor of this soup depends, to a large extent, on the quality of the stock, so it's a good idea to either make your own (see Chicken Stock in miscellaneous and substitute beef bones for chicken) or buy the best quality available. For this soup, whipped smooth in the blender, there is no need to peel the carrots, just give them a good scrub.

2 tbsp. butter
1 medium onion, chopped
1 lb. carrots, sliced
1 qt. beef stock
Salt and pepper, to taste
¼ cup natural yogurt
1 tsp. fresh thyme, chopped

Sauté the onion in butter until translucent, add the carrots and stock, and cook until the carrots are soft. Cool to lukewarm. Add salt, pepper, and yogurt and whip in the blender until smooth.

Serve either hot or cold sprinkled with chopped thyme.

Serves 4.

Lasanha de Berinjela
Eggplant Lasagna

Eggplant is quite popular in São Paulo and frequently appears in hors d'oeuvres. This substantial dish makes a tasty lunch, accompanied only by a tossed salad.

1 1-lb. eggplant, cut crosswise into ¼-½-inch slices
Vegetable oil
1 ½ cups (about) tomato sauce, either homemade or purchased
3 oz. ham, chopped
10 oz. mozzarella, sliced
3 eggs, fried, the yolks beginning to set
½ lb. Parmesan, freshly grated

Heat the oven to 350 degrees F. Brush both sides of the eggplant with oil.

Arrange in a single layer on a baking sheet and roast in the oven until soft and brown on one side, about 5-8 minutes. Turn and repeat on the other side. Remove from the oven

Oil an ovenproof casserole dish; for this amount, I have found an 8x3 inch round bowl is perfect. Thinly spread a little tomato sauce on the bottom, then layer the ham, mozzarella, eggplant, and more sauce. Continue layering in this order, arranging the eggs on the last layer of mozzarella. Top with a final layer of eggplant, the remainder of the sauce, and spread with Parmesan. Return the dish to the oven and bake until the cheese is golden, about 30 minutes.

Serves 3.

Pão de Batata
Potato Bread or Rolls

In general, Brazilians are not great fans of potatoes, other than French fries, and they much prefer rice dishes. However, the Potato Roll is a favorite snack of everyone, for sale in bakeries, supermarkets, and in kiosks in the malls. At home, they are good right out of the oven with herb butter or as mini sandwiches with your own filling.

    1 cup warm (110-115 degrees) milk
    3 tbsp. sugar
    3 tbsp. yeast
    1 lb. potatoes, peeled, cooked, mashed, and cooled
    1 cup warm water
    3 large eggs
    ½ cup corn oil
    2 tbsp. salt
    10-15 cups (approximately 2 lb.) flour

Combine milk and sugar in a large bowl, add yeast, and let it dissolve and bubble for 10 minutes. Add next five ingredients, mix thoroughly, and stir in ½ the flour, gradually adding more until the dough leaves the sides of the bowl. Turn out on a board or table and knead for 10 minutes, adding more flour, if necessary, to keep the dough from sticking to the table. Form the dough into a ball and put it in a large, greased bowl, turning the dough over so that all sides

are greased. Cover the bowl with a clean towel and set it to rise in a warm area until double in bulk—about 1 hour. Knead again briefly and form into rolls or two loaves, each in an 8-inch round baking pan. Let rise again for 20-30 minutes covered with the towel. Bake at 350 degrees F for 50 minutes to 1 hour for loaves and approximately 20 minutes for rolls.

Makes 2 loaves or 50 rolls.

Trancoise
Trancoise

This cold soup, another creation of Chef Quentin Geenen de Saint Maur and included in his book *Muito Prazer, Brasil,* is actually a sweet potato vichyssoise. When buying the potatoes, choose the very light yellow or white ones.

5 cups chicken stock, free of any fat
12 oz. sweet potatoes, peeled and cut in pieces
1 small onion, chopped
1 cup half-and-half or whole milk
1 cup natural yogurt
Salt and pepper, to taste
¼ cup parsley, chopped
Salt and pepper, to taste
1 tbsp. red peppercorns, freshly ground

Bring the chicken stock to a boil and add the potatoes and onion, lower the fire, cover, and cook until the potatoes are soft. Add the half-and-half, cool, and add the yogurt. Whirl in the blender until smooth and taste for seasoning. Chill for several hours and serve very cold, sprinkled with chopped parsley and ground red peppercorns.

Serves 6 to 8.

6

Coco/Coconut

The coconut stand is small—really just a cart—but as one of the few places where freshly grated coconut meat can be purchased, it is an essential part of the feira. The importance of coconut in Brazilian cuisine cannot be too highly stressed, as it is included in every type of dish, from fish to chicken to vegetable to fruit recipes. North Americans are often confused by *coco gelado,* green coconuts from which clear, slightly sweet water is drunk, as opposed to the coconut milk used in recipes. In this hot climate, the former, believed to have great health benefits, is more popular and much more refreshing than soft drinks, and there are tiny stands all over Brazil where whole coconuts may be purchased for less than a dollar. At each stand, the vendor is armed with a long, very sharp machete, and while holding the smooth-skinned green globe in one hand, he chops the hard top in a "v" or slashes a straight shallow cut before inserting a straw and handing the *coco gelado* to the customer. Although the vendor appears to be relaxed and is often

very chatty during this maneuver, I have never been able to watch that descending machete without severe terror and breathless foreboding, knowing that one tiny miscalculation would result in missing fingers or the loss of a hand. Nor am I reassured by the fact that I've never heard of this happening or noticed a significant proportion of the population with one useless hand. Although I love this fresh, natural beverage on a hot day, I do look the other way while the vendor prepares my coconut.

In the feira, only hairy, brown coconuts are in evidence, and the utensil used by the vendor to grate the white meat of the halved fruit with lightening speed is, unlike the lethal, dangerous machete, a small tool, similar in appearance to a vegetable peeler. Grated coconut is available in two sizes, which are measured in plastic glasses: the large-size glass appears roughly equivalent to a ten-ounce container and the smaller is like a jelly jar. Even in the refrigerator, freshly grated coconut spoils within a few days, so I keep it in the freezer. Since fresh coconut is often unavailable in the U.S. and difficult and time-consuming to grate when it is found, packaged grated coconut will work perfectly in these recipes as long as it is unsweetened.

Pudim de Queijo Parmesão com Leite de Coco
Flan with Cheese and Coconut Milk

Flans of all kinds are enormously popular in São Paulo and usually appear on restaurant menus and at buffets as well as at home for dessert. Americans make flans or baked custards with whole milk, but in Brazil, they are made with sweetened condensed milk. An unusual variation in this recipe is the Parmesan cheese, which must be freshly grated.

Caramel Sauce
1 cup sugar
½ cup hot water

Flan
4 large eggs
1 cup coconut milk
1 can sweetened condensed milk
¾ cup milk
2 oz. grated Parmesan cheese
Toasted grated coconut

Caramel Sauce
Combine sugar and hot water in a saucepan and cook, over very low heat, until the sugar melts and turns copper color. Pour into a metal loaf pan or a flan pan and set aside.

Flan
Mix all the ingredients, except the toasted coconut, in a blender and pour into the caramel-lined pan. Place pan in a larger pan with hot water reaching halfway up the side of the flan pan. Bake in a 350-degree oven for 35 minutes or until a table knife inserted in the center comes out almost clean. Immediately remove from the hot water bath and immerse the pan in cool water to stop the cooking process; the flan will become increasingly firm as it cools. Chill in the refrigerator for 4 hours or overnight. Just before serving, garnish with toasted coconut.

Serves 8.

Torta de Coco com Creme de Maracujá
Coconut Pie with Passion Fruit Cream

It is important that fresh pulp with seeds be used in this cream as the seeds add a textural contrast, while the flavor of fresh passion fruit has much more tang than the bottled juice.

Crust
1½ cups flour
¼ tsp. salt
⅓ cup sugar
½ cup unsalted butter
3 large egg yolks

Filling
⅓ cup sugar
1 large egg
1 large egg yolk
½ tsp. lime zest
⅔ cup whipping cream
½ cup unsweetened coconut milk
3 tbsp. fresh lemon or lime juice
1¼ cups grated unsweetened coconut

Passion Fruit Cream
¾ cup heavy whipping cream
½ cup sugar
⅓ cup sour cream
5 tbsp. passion fruit pulp

Crust

Mix the flour, salt, and sugar in the food processor or by hand using a wire pastry blender, add the butter, and pulse until coarse meal forms. Add egg yolks and process until clumps form. Gather the dough and press it onto the bottom and up about 1 inch inside a 9-inch spring-form pan. Chill 1 hour. Preheat oven to 400 degrees and bake 12 minutes or till lightly colored. Cool completely.

Filling

Preheat oven to 325 degrees. Beat the sugar, egg, egg yolk, and lime zest in large bowl for 1 minute. Stir in the whipping cream, coconut milk, and lime juice. When all the ingredients are well blended, add the shredded coconut. Pour into the crust and bake until set in center and golden, about 40 minutes. Cool completely, then chill.

Passion Fruit Cream

Whisk cream, sugar, and sour cream in medium bowl until thickened. Pulse passion fruit pulp briefly in the blender and then strain to obtain the juice. Reserve a few seeds. Add the juice to the cream mixture and whisk until peaks form. Add the reserved seeds and give the mixture a few more whisks to incorporate.

To Serve

Cut in wedges and add a large dollop of passion fruit cream.

Serves 8.

Pudim de Coco e Molho de Manga e Moranga
Coconut Pudding with Mango and Strawberry Sauce

This delightfully refreshing summer dessert is quick to make and has no complicated ingredients. Perfect for a dinner party, the three components may be made the day before, covered, and refrigerated separately until just before serving time.

Pudding

½ cup sugar
1 tbsp. cornstarch
1 ½ cups milk
1 tbsp. plus 1 tsp. of gelatin
¼ cup water
1 cup coconut milk

Mango Sauce
1 mango
1 tbsp. rum

Strawberry Sauce
½ lb. strawberries
⅓ cup sugar
1 tbsp. rum

Pudding
Mix the sugar, cornstarch, and milk, bring to a boil, and remove from the heat. Soak the gelatin in water and add to the hot milk, stirring to dissolve. Add the coconut milk and divide among 6 individual molds. Cool and refrigerate.

Sauces
For both the mango sauce and the strawberry sauce, purée in the blender and chill.

To Serve
Just before serving, remove the three components from the refrigerator and unmold the pudding on individual serving plates. Pour mango sauce on one side of each pudding and the strawberry sauce on the other.

Serves 6.

Manjar de Coco com Compota de Ameixa Preta
Coconut Delicacy with Prune Compote

Lenina Pomeranz, who also provided the recipe for Guava Tart, submitted the recipe for this traditional dessert.

1 can condensed milk
1 small bottle coconut milk (about 1 cup)
2 cups milk
3 tbsp. sugar
1 tsp. vanilla extract
2 rounded tbsp. cornstarch
8 oz. grated unsweetened coconut

Compote

3½ oz. prunes without pits
2 tbsp. sugar
1½ cups water
1 stick cinnamon
Juice of ½ lemon or lime

Mix the condensed milk, coconut milk, 1 cup milk, sugar, and vanilla in a saucepan. In a small bowl, mix the remaining milk and cornstarch. When the cornstarch is dissolved, add to the ingredients in the saucepan. Stirring, bring to a boil. Lower the heat and continue to cook until very thick, stirring constantly with a wooden spoon to prevent sticking. Take off the fire and reserve.

Lightly grease a metal mold and pour in half the cooked mixture. Add the coconut to the remaining half and pour into the mold. Cool and refrigerate.

Compote

Combine all the ingredients, bring to a boil, and cook over a very low fire for 30-40 minutes. It should be thick but still spreadable. Allow to cool to room temperature.

To Serve

Unmold the *manjar* and cover with the compote.

Serves 10-15.

Pão de Cenoura e Coco
Carrot Coconut Bread

A cross between cake and bread, this is a delightful breakfast treat for the holidays or Sunday mornings. Because the recipe is a large one, it's a good one for guests and can be served either warm or cold.

½ tsp. salt
1 tsp. baking soda
1 tsp. baking powder
1 tsp. cinnamon
1 cup sugar

2 ½ cups flour
3 eggs
½ cup milk
½ cup oil
2 cups grated carrots
1¼ cups grated unsweetened coconut
½ cup light raisins
½ cup cashew, walnuts, or pecan, chopped

Mix the dry ingredients. Add the eggs, milk, and oil and beat smooth. Add the carrots, coconut, and raisins and beat again. Stir in the nuts and turn into a buttered 14x10-inch pan. Bake at 400 degrees for 40 minutes or until the bread tests done.

Serves 8.

Quindim
Quindim

This super rich dessert with a Bantu name is one of the culinary trademarks of Brazil. More than likely the dish was created in the seventeenth century by African slaves in the Brazilian northeast, where there was an abundance of both coconuts and sugarcane, to please their Portuguese masters who loved desserts with lots of eggs. *Quindim* may be baked in individual portions using muffin tins, custard cups, or ceramic molds, or as a pie in a mold with a hole in the center. In the latter case, it is called *Quindão*. Innumerable variations of this recipe exist; Lenina Pomeranz provided this particular version.

13 egg yolks
1½ cups sugar
3 tbsp. butter, melted
2¼ cups grated unsweetened coconut
1 tsp. vanilla extract
Butter for coating the molds

Beat the egg yolks with the sugar and butter. Add the coconut and vanilla and beat again. Since this is a very rich dessert, choose small muffin tins or molds with ⅓ cup or less capacity. Butter the molds, sprinkle the bottoms and sides with sugar, pour in the batter, and lower the molds into a larger pan of hot water. Bake at 350 degrees for 40-60 minutes, until firm or a toothpick comes out clean when inserted in the center and the surface golden. The cooking time will depend on the type of mold you have selected. Cool to lukewarm and unmold; they will stick if you try to do this when they are cold. If you have used a muffin pan, run a sharp knife around the edge of only 1 *quindim*, turn the pan over and, holding your hand under the cup, unmold. Repeat the process. Do not try to unmold all of them together as some are likely to slip and land on one side. Chill.

Serves 10-12, depending on size of the mold.

Cocada
Cocada

There are many recipes for this traditional sweet. The most familiar form is a round ball peddled in wax-paper-lined baskets at the beach by men and women who have made them at home. This variation may be baked in individual ramekins or in a round ovenproof dish and is equally good eaten hot or chilled.

> 1 generous cup grated unsweetened coconut
> 3 eggs
> 3 cups sugar
> 1 scant cup milk
> 2 tbsp. butter
> 8 oz. milk chocolate, broken into smallish pieces

Combine all the ingredients except the chocolate. Butter an 8-inch round pan or ovenproof dish and pour in the mixture. Add the chocolate and delicately stir to mix. Bake at 350 degrees for about 30 minutes.

Serves 6.

7

Bananas

Every feira has stand after stand of banana vendors, all selling more or less the same produce for very little money. Probably originating in southwest Asia, the banana has now spread throughout all tropical and subtropical areas of the globe, and this fruit is so common and cheap in Brazil that a rock-bottom price in shops or industry is referred to as a "banana price."

Often considered the perfect fruit, there are many varieties of bananas in Brazil, ranging from the tiny *ouro* (gold) to the large, all-purpose *nanica*, and they appear in countless dishes. Easy to digest, this fruit can be eaten by anyone, including infants, the elderly, and the infirm.

Traditionally, the leaves of the banana plant are used to wrap and/or cover certain foods during the cooking period, especially over an open fire. In the more rural areas of the country, this method is still used. Another Brazilian practice of many years is to rub banana peels on mosquito bites, instantly dispelling the itch.

Sopa de Banana Com Curry
Curried Banana Soup

When I have too many ripe or over-ripe bananas and must use them immediately, this dish is a welcome alternative to banana bread or cake. It's easy, quick, and loved by everyone. Although the recipe calls for cream, I usually serve this as a first course and substitute whole milk, which makes a lighter soup. As a supper dish accompanied by a light salad, the cream would be more suitable. Although it keeps perfectly in the refrigerator for a day or two, this soup cannot be successfully frozen.

3 tbsp. butter
1½ cups chopped onions
2 tsp. hot curry powder
2½ qt. chicken broth, preferably homemade
2 lb. ripe bananas, sliced
⅓ cup lime juice (lemon may be used)
Salt, to taste
2 cups light cream
Parsley, finely chopped

Melt the butter in a large pan and sauté the onions for 5 minutes. Add the curry powder and cook for 30 seconds longer. Add the chicken broth,

bananas, lime juice, and salt. Bring to a boil, lower the heat, cover with a lid, and cook for 15 minutes. Cool to lukewarm, whirl in the blender until smooth, taste for salt, and add the cream. Serve very hot with a sprinkling of finely chopped parsley.

Serves 10.

Farofa de Banana
Banana *Farofa*

In its most basic form, *farofa* is a dish usually made from finely ground manioc meal, toasted in a dry skillet or with butter or oil, and sprinkled over just about everything. However, *farofas* can be quite elaborate and involve a number of ingredients; this particular recipe is unusual and more sophisticated because it uses cornmeal rather than manioc meal. *Malagueta* pepper, a small, potent pepper that is probably not readily available in the U.S., is used in this dish, but other chilies may be substituted with only a slight difference in flavor.

3 tbsp. butter
8 bananas, sliced
1½ cups cornmeal
Salt
Chilies, minced, to taste

Melt the butter, add the bananas, and sauté for 5 minutes on low heat. Add the cornmeal, salt, and chilies, mix well, remove from the heat, and serve immediately.

Serves 6-7.

Creme de Banana com Limoncello
Banana Cream with Limoncello

This light and sophisticated dessert is a perfect example of the influence that immigrants—in this case Italian—have had on indigenous ingredients. An ideal alternative to an ice cream finale on a hot summer day, this is also a very welcome ending to a large meal at any time of the year.

1 envelope of plain gelatin
⅓ cup water
4 medium-size, ripe bananas
¾ cup limoncello
Juice of 1 lemon
2 cups heavy cream
Slices of lemon
Mint leaves

In a small bowl, soak the gelatin in water for a few minutes. Meanwhile, mix the bananas, limoncello, and lemon juice in the blender to form a smooth cream. Dissolve the gelatin over hot water and add to the banana mixture, blending on high speed for a few seconds. Beat the cream until soft peaks form and then carefully fold together with the banana mixture. Distribute in individual bowls—sherbet glasses are ideal—and refrigerate. At serving time, decorate with thin slices of lemon and mint leaves.

Serves 6-8.

Torta de Banana ao Forno
Hot Banana Pie

Brazilians love *tortas,* or pies, both savory and sweet. Unlike pies in the United States, there is no standard crust and sometimes, as in this case, they are without a crust at all. The bananas should be very lightly sautéed since they will be further cooked in the oven.

5 eggs, separated
¾ cup sugar
6 bananas, cut in fairly thick slices
¼ tsp. cream of tartar
Heavy cream

Heat the oven to 325 degrees. Separate the egg yolks and whites. With an electric beater, beat the yolks and ¼ cup sugar until thick and lemon-colored. Turn into a buttered, round, 9-inch pie or tart plate, slip into the oven, and bake until the surface is slightly firm to the touch, about 20 minutes.

Meanwhile, sauté the bananas and beat the egg whites until frothy. Add the cream of tartar, beat again, and, continuing to beat at high speed, gradually add the remaining ½ cup sugar. Remove the pie dish from the oven, lower the oven heat to 300 degrees, and scatter the bananas over the egg yolk base. Top with beaten egg whites, lifting them into attractive peaks. Bake until the egg whites are golden brown, about another 20 minutes. Serve hot with heavy cream.

Serves 6.

Arroz com Bananas
Rice with Bananas

This is a delicious and unusual dish that conveniently makes use of a small amount of leftover chicken. Cooked bananas do not stand up well, so plan to eat this dish in one meal with nothing left for tomorrow's lunch.

6 medium to small bananas
1 cup chicken, cooked, deboned, and shredded
1½ cups tomato sauce
2 tbsp. green olives, seeded and sliced
2 tbsp. seedless black grapes
1 green apple, peeled and cut in small cubes
1 small can of corn, drained
3 cups of rice, cooked
½ lb. mozzarella, cut in slices

Peel the bananas, cut in half, and fry in hot oil. Drain on paper towels and reserve. Combine the chicken, tomato sauce, olives, grapes, apple, and corn. Add the rice and mix well. In a greased, ovenproof casserole or baking dish, layer the rice mixture, sautéed bananas, and mozzarella, ending with the mozzarella. Cover with a lid or aluminum foil and heat in a moderate oven for about 20 minutes or until the dish is hot and the cheese melted.

Serves 6-8.

Pão de Banana Mel
Banana Honey Bread

This raisin loaf is a far cry from the banana breads usually baked in the U.S. and exemplifies the affinity Brazilians have with both bananas and honey. Jars of honey are sold in feiras, supermarkets, and open-air stands along the highways in areas where beekeepers collect and bottle honey. *Propolis*, collected by bees and used in construction of the hive, is used by Brazilians in traditional medicine.

⅔ cup warm water
1 tbsp. sugar
2 packages yeast
1 egg
2 tbsp. vegetable oil
¼ cup honey
2 very ripe, medium-size bananas, well mashed
1 tsp. salt
1 tsp. cinnamon
4½ cups (about) flour
1 cup raisins, either light or dark
½ cup Brazil nuts or walnuts, chopped

Combine the water, sugar, and yeast in a large bowl and allow to rest for 5-10 minutes or until slightly puffy. Combine this mixture with the egg, vegetable oil, honey, bananas, salt, and cinnamon. Then add the flour, beginning with 3 cups and gradually adding more as needed. Turn out on a table or board and knead for 10 minutes, adding more flour as necessary to prevent sticking. After 5 minutes, knead in the raisins and nuts. Form the bread into a ball, place in a buttered bowl, turning to grease all surfaces, cover with a towel, and let rise until double in bulk. Punch down, knead briefly, and form into a loaf. Place in a buttered 5x7-inch loaf pan, let rise again, and bake at 350 degrees for 45 minutes or until done. Turn onto a rack, cover with a towel, and cool.

Makes 1 loaf.

Purê de Banana
Banana Purée

This simple purée often accompanies fish, chicken, and meats. Even though the plantain is a member of the banana family and in Portuguese is called *banana de terra* (despite the fact that it grows on trees like every other banana), this dish should never be called plantain puree.

3 ripe plantains
1 tbsp. butter
1 tbsp. grated Parmesan cheese
¼ cup or more milk

Scrub the plantains and place them, unpeeled, in a large pot or skillet. Cover with water and boil until the skins open or are very soft—about 20

Bananas

minutes. Peel, remove any black seeds, and blend in the processor or blender with the butter, Parmesan, and sufficient milk to bring the mixture to a purée consistency. Turn into a saucepan and cook over a low fire, stirring constantly, until it comes to a boil. Remove from the fire and serve.

Serves 4 or 5.

Bananas Recheadas com Coco
Bananas Stuffed with Coconut

This dessert is easily made and delicious, but be careful when opening the bananas as the skins will become the serving dishes.

6 medium-size bananas
2 cups heavy cream
6 tbsp. sugar
7 oz. grated unsweetened coconut

With a sharp knife, slit the banana skins from top to bottom and very gently press open. Using a spoon, remove the banana flesh and mash with a fork. Beat the cream, add the sugar, and continue beating until peaks form. Mix the cream, mashed bananas, and coconut and fill the banana skins. Serve immediately.

Serves 6.

8

Meat

Legally, meat cannot be sold in a street feira, but since it is an extremely important item in Brazilian cuisine, it should certainly be included in any cookbook of the country. Until recently, Brazilians didn't consider a meal complete and satisfactory if it failed to include some form of meat. Beef is by far the most popular, followed closely by pork, but the cuts of both bear no resemblance to those in the U.S. For some reason that I cannot fathom, lamb and veal are almost unobtainable in Brazilian markets, although they are occasionally featured in chic French restaurants in São Paulo. When it does appear in a butcher shop or supermarket, lamb is nearly always a leg, sold frozen, and is imported from New Zealand despite the fact that sheep farms are common in Argentina, Chile, Uruguay, Peru, and southern Brazil.

Most meat markets carry whole or half hams only at Christmas. However, ham, sliced paper thin, is very popular, available everywhere, and used in a variety of dishes as well as in sandwiches. I have never seen ham steaks,

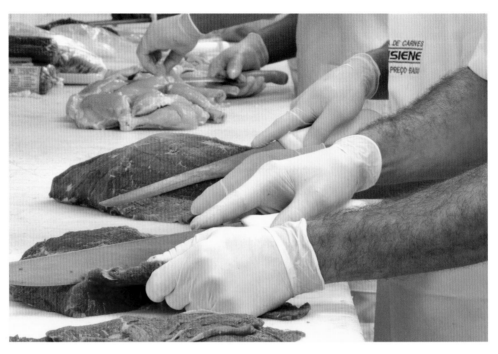

which are ideal for an average-sized family, at any time of year, but I can always find an infinite variety of sausages. These do not appear in patty form but are in casings, both small and large, and are often barbecued, thickly sliced, and served with cocktails.

Canapé de Carne
Meat Canapé

This hors d'oeuvre is not difficult, but all the preparation should be complete before the guests arrive with only the broiling or sautéing of the meat left to the last minute. Although you may cut and toast your own bread rounds, it's fiddly, time-consuming work. I suggest buying packaged toast rounds about 1 ½ inches in diameter or slightly bigger.

1 lb. lean ground beef
1 cup diced bacon, loosely packed and fried
¼ tsp. garlic, minced
2 tsp. hot pepper flakes, or to taste
Salt and pepper, to taste
Bananas, cut in ¼-inch slices

Lemon juice
Toast rounds

Combine ground meat with fried bacon, garlic, pepper flakes, salt, and pepper. Form into flat, bite-sized patties, ¼ inch thick and slightly smaller than the toast rounds. Cut as many slices of bananas as there are patties and marinate in lemon juice. Broil the patties until brown, then turn and brown the other side. Arrange the toasts on a serving platter and, while the patties broil, place a slice of banana on each. Top with a nicely browned patty. It's important to serve these immediately.

Serves about 18.

Carne de Panela de Gaúcho
Gaucho Pot Roast

In Brazil, the term *Gaucho* refers to someone who is from the state of Rio Grande do Sul, a region known for its cattle. Not surprisingly, the cuisine of that area focuses on beef and pork dishes and stems from the culinary traditions of the cowboys who roam the prairies and tend the cattle.

2 lb. rump roast, trimmed of fat and gristle
Ground black pepper
1 tbsp. oil
3 thick slices bacon, chopped
1 onion, chopped
2 cloves garlic, minced
¼ cup wine vinegar
1 cup water (approximately)
Salt, to taste

Rub the roast with pepper and brown it on all sides in the oil. Meanwhile, fry the bacon. When it is brown, drain off most of the fat and sauté the onions and garlic until transparent. Add the bacon, onions, and garlic to the browned meat. Combine the vinegar and water, pour over the roast, cover, and cook over a low fire for about 2 hours or until tender. Add water from time to time, if necessary, as the cooking liquid will be the sauce. Taste for salt; the bacon makes it unlikely that any will be needed.

Serves 4.

Meat

Carne Seca Com Abóbora
Dried Beef and Squash

Maria de Fatima Honorato, originally from Minas Gerais but a São Paulo resident for many years, has developed this recipe and assured me that the amounts given here serve four, but they can be successfully doubled and quadrupled for a large group. She suggests using a ripe, yellow-orange acorn squash, as others may be more watery. The final product should be a mashed squash, like mashed potatoes, with the shredded beef in it.

1 lb. *carne seca* (dried beef), cut in large squares
2-4 tbsp. vegetable oil
2 cloves garlic, minced
1 onion, chopped
Hot red peppers, to taste, minced (optional)
½ cup parsley, chopped
½ large acorn squash, peeled, seeded, and diced
Salt and pepper, to taste

Soak the beef overnight, changing the water 2-4 times. Cook in fresh water to cover until it is so tender it almost falls apart. Shred the meat and brown lightly in oil with the garlic, onions, and peppers; do not overly brown or it will be hard and dry. Add the parsley and squash, cover, and cook until the squash is mushy, adding a little water if necessary. When done, mash and taste for salt and pepper.

Serves 4.

Arroz de Carreteiro
Prairie Rice

In Brazil, dried meat, alternately called *carne seca, charque,* and *carne do sol,* depending on the location in the country and the way it is dried, is usually beef or occasionally pork that has been salted either in brine or in salt and dried in a rigidly prescribed manner for five days. When exported, it is sometimes called jerked beef. Unlike beef jerky, which is cut into strips and cured in an entirely different manner, *carne seca* is cured in blocks. Because the salt content is so high, the meat must be soaked overnight in water that is changed three or four times, before it can be cooked. Then it must be boiled in fresh water for about three hours or until fork tender, after which it is shredded or cubed. Now it is ready for use in a variety of dishes. Devoted to their pressure cookers, Brazilians invariably choose this shorter cooking method when dealing with *carne seca*, but I, like most Americans here, are wary of a utensil that can explode and prefer to simmer the meat. *Carne seca* can be ordered through the Internet sites in the sources section at the back of this book.

    1 tbsp. oil
    3 oz. hot sausage, chopped
    1 large onion, peeled and chopped
    5 medium tomatoes, peeled and chopped
    2 green peppers, cubed
    4 tbsp. chopped parsley
    2 tsp. fresh basil, or 1 tsp. dried basil
    1 bay leaf
    4 tbsp. chopped green onion
    Salt and pepper, to taste
    3 cups beef stock, homemade, canned, or made with a beef cube
    1½ cups rice
    1 lb. *carne seca*, soaked and boiled as described above and shredded

Fry the sausage, onions, tomatoes, and green peppers in oil for about 5 minutes. Add the parsley, basil, bay leaf, and green onion. Mix well and taste for salt and pepper. Bring the beef broth to a boil. Add well-washed rice to the meat mixture and fry for 30 seconds to coat the grains of rice with oil, then add boiling beef broth and the shredded *carne seca*. Cover and cook on medium heat for about 15 minutes until rice is *al dente*.

This dish can be served on a platter with fried bananas or plantains on the side. Cut bananas lengthwise and fry in butter until golden.

Serves 6.

Escondidinho
Hidden Meat Casserole

This is one of the most delicious of the many *carne seca* dishes in Brazil and is worth the search for both the dried meat and the fresh manioc. If the latter is not

available, mashed potatoes may be substituted although the flavor will not be the same. For unusual ingredients, check Latino markets or refer to the sources guide.

1 lb. *carne seca* (dried beef)
3 tbsp. olive oil
2 medium onions, finely chopped
2 tbsp. parsley
2 lb. fresh manioc, or yucca, cut in 1-inch pieces
1 cup unsweetened coconut milk
Salt, to taste
1 cup grated Parmesan cheese

Prepare the meat by soaking and cooking as explained in the previous recipe (Prairie Rice). When it is soft, cut it in small cubes and cook with the olive oil and onion until the onion is golden. Add the parsley, mix well, and set aside.

Preheat the oven to 350 degrees. Cook the manioc in water and ½-cup coconut milk. When soft like a boiled potato, strain and reserve the liquid. Cool the manioc, remove any tough fibers, and either mash with a potato masher or whip in the blender with ½-cup coconut milk and enough reserved cooking liquid to bring it to the consistency of mashed potatoes. Taste for salt, but remember that the meat is still salty.

Grease a 9x13-inch casserole. Spread half the manioc purée on the bottom, put all the meat on top, and finish with another layer of purée. Sprinkle cheese on top and cook for 30 minutes.

Serves 6.

Feijoada
Feijoada

This is the national dish of Brazil and originated in the kitchens of Bahia, where slaves used the dried beans and scraps of meat they were given to create a feast in celebration of the African gods they had brought with them to the new world. Despite the fact that there are now endless variations of the *feijoada,* its basic components are smoked and dried meat, black beans, and accompaniments including hot peppers, kale, toasted manioc meal, and oranges. *Feijoada* is a heavy meal and always served midday and, in São Paulo, only on Saturday and Wednesday.

I have been served this particular version of *feijoada* many times in the home of Susie Lund, a resident of São Paulo for nearly half a century. Over the years, she has collaborated with Dona Teta, Dona Anita, and, during the last decade, Dona Marlice Bach to develop this recipe. Two of Susie's adult children now live in the U.S., and even though this is a labor-intensive undertaking, once a year they and their friends get together, divide up the tasks, and cook a *feijoada*. This is an elaborate recipe, and if some of the ingredients aren't available, eliminate them and tailor the dish to what you have—just as the Brazilians have done ever since the *feijoada* was invented. Be sure it includes black beans, *carne seca*, sausage, and some of the above listed accompaniments.

2¼ lb. *carne seca* or uncooked dried beef (not beef jerky)
2¼ lb. black beans
3½ lb. smoked pork loin
2¼ lb. pork loin
1 tongue
1 smoked rack of ribs (optional)
1 rack of ribs
1 pig's foot (optional)
1 pig's ear (optional)
1 pig's tail (optional)
2 sausages, Italian style if available
½ lb. pork sausage without pepper
½ lb. Portuguese sausage
1 package bacon
2½ lb. ripe tomatoes, chopped
2 lb. onions, chopped
1 clove garlic, chopped
1 bunch parsley, chopped
Pinch of cumin
½ cup *cachaça*
½ cup orange juice
3 cups uncooked rice

Thursday evening: Soak the *carne seca* overnight (**not** the smoked meat or sausage). Change the water twice. Wash the beans and soak overnight in a separate container.

Friday: Trim the fat from the soaked meat, allow it to drain, and place in a large pot. Cover with water, bring to a boil, and cook until tender. In another pot, bring the beans to a boil in the water in which they were soaked.

Cook for 1 hour and add the *carne seca* and all the other meats except the bacon. Continue to cook until all the meats are tender, which will probably be around 3 hours. The tail, tongue, ear, and foot, if used, are only included for flavor and thickening of the beans and are not served with the final dish. Fry the bacon, crumble, and reserve for the kale.

In a separate pan, sauté the tomatoes, onions, garlic, parsley, and cumin. When the meat and bean mixture is almost cooked, add the tomato mixture. With a slotted spoon, remove a large amount of beans, mash, and return them to the pot. Cook for half an hour, then remove from the fire and allow to cool.

Saturday: Remove any fat that has risen to the top. Simmer the beans and meat on a low fire to thicken, taking care not to allow them to stick to the bottom of the pot. Add the *cachaça* and orange juice. Cook the rice according to the directions in chapter 1. At serving time, discard the tongue, foot, ear, and tail, if used, and remove the remaining meat. Arrange the meats, sliced, on a ceramic serving platter and serve the beans and rice in other dishes.

Feijoada is traditionally accompanied by one or all of the following:

1. *Malagueta* pepper sauce or other hot pepper sauce
2. Kale, very finely sliced and sautéed in chopped garlic and oil and mixed with fried bacon
3. Manioc meal, toasted and salted
4. Sautéed bananas
5. Navel oranges, peeled and separated into sections

Serves 12-15.

Maria Rita
Maria Rita

No one seems to know the identity of Maria Rita, but her legacy was this recipe, which has made its way into the majority of Brazilian homes, cookbooks, and countless buffet tables. This simple dish is distinguished by the addition of cabbage.

2 tbsp. oil
8 oz. ground beef
1 onion, chopped
1 large tomato, chopped
2 cloves garlic, minced
1 cup rice

2 cups water
2-3 large cabbage leaves
Salt, to taste

In a pan with a lid, heat the oil and add the beef. When it loses its raw appearance, add the onion, tomato, and garlic. Continue to cook for 5-10 minutes or until the onion is translucent and the tomato is soft. Sir in the rice, add 2 cups of water, and mix well. Cook, covered, for about 20 minutes or until the rice tests done. Meanwhile, cut the cabbage leaves into medium-size pieces. Turn off the fire under the Maria Rita, stir in the cabbage leaves, and allow the dish to rest, covered, for a few minutes while the cabbage wilts. Serve immediately over rice.

Serves 3-4.

Picadinho
Picadinho

This is a classic Brazilian stew that, like *carne seca* and *bacalhau,* is sometimes glamorized by serving in a baked, round squash. If you choose such a presentation, select a squash weighing 3 to 4 pounds, cut a round lid from the squash, clean

Meat

out the seeds and fibers, and add ½ cup of salted stock. Replace the lid and bake at 350 degrees in a greased pan for around 1 hour or until the flesh is tender but the shell is still firm. Drain the squash, fill it with the *picadinho,* and, when serving, scoop out some squash with the meat. Variations of the stew are endless; ground beef may be substituted for steak, pitted green and black olives may be added to the meat mixture, and the dish may be made without hot peppers. Sautéed bananas are a common accompaniment as are poached eggs.

1¾ lb. good-quality steak
3 tomatoes
1 red bell pepper
1 green bell pepper
Olive oil
1 onion, chopped
4 cloves garlic, minced
¼ cup tomato sauce
2 hot chili peppers, or to taste
½ cup water, vegetable, or meat stock
¼ cup parsley, chopped
Salt to taste

Slice the steak very thinly and cut in small cubes. Peel, seed, and coarsely chop the tomatoes. Seed the bell peppers and then cube. Heat a minimum of oil in a large skillet and quickly brown the meat, then remove and reserve. If necessary, add more oil and lightly brown the onion and garlic and add the bell peppers, tomatoes, tomato sauce, chili peppers, and stock. Cover and simmer for 10 minutes. Add the steak, parsley, and salt and simmer, uncovered, for 20 minutes or until the liquid is nearly absorbed. Serve with rice, hot pepper sauce, and sautéed bananas.

Serves 6. If in a squash, serves 8.

Paella do Rio Grande do Sul
Paella of Rio Grande do Sul

Though only vaguely related to paella, this attractive dish is delicious and should be presented in a wide, shallow serving bowl. If either leftover cooked pork or chicken is available, it may be cubed and added with the onion and garlic.

Vegetable oil for sautéing
¼ lb. lean pork, cubed
¼ lb. chicken, cubed
¼ lb. sausage, sliced
1 onion, chopped
1 clove garlic, minced
1 tbsp. tomato extract
2 cups cooked rice
1 large tomato, sliced
½ green bell pepper, chopped
½ red bell pepper, chopped
½ yellow bell pepper, chopped
3 tbsp. chopped parsley
Scallions, chopped

Sauté the pork, chicken, and sausage separately; remove from the pan and reserve. Adding oil if necessary, sauté the onion and garlic in the same pan and add the tomato extract. Cook for 1 minute and add the rice and meat. Add the tomatoes, bell peppers, and parsley and cook for a few more minutes, adding a little water if necessary. The peppers should be crunchy but not raw. Turn into a wide-serving dish and sprinkle with scallions.

Serves 4.

Mexidão Mineiro
Mineiro Mix

As the title indicates, this is a dish originally from the state of Minas Gerais and is ideal for a busy day. Except for the eggs, it can be prepared ahead of time and then reheated while the eggs fry.

½ lb. Italian-style sausage, sliced
4 slices bacon, chopped (about 3 ounces)
1 onion, thinly sliced
4 cloves garlic, minced
2 cups cooked pinto beans, well drained
1 tomato, chopped
3 cups white rice, cooked
Salt, to taste
Hot chili sauce, or minced chili peppers
¼-½ cup chopped scallions, including some of the green part
4 eggs, fried

Sauté the sausage, using a little oil if necessary. When it begins to brown, add the bacon and cook until crisp. Pour out most of the fat, add onion and garlic, and cook until the onion is transparent. Add the beans and tomato, cook for a few minutes, and stir in the rice. Taste for salt, add chili sauce or minced hot peppers to taste, and turn onto a platter. Sprinkle with scallions and top with the eggs.

Serves 4.

Lombo com Cebolas e Alho
Pork Roast with Onions and Garlic

As a working mother with two pre-teenage boys, Laura de Borba welcomes dishes that can be expanded to accommodate unexpected guests, are not labor intensive, and cook in a short period of time. This roast, which she developed, meets those requirements and creates its own sauce while cooking. As with any roast, especially pork, a meat thermometer is mandatory to eliminate guesswork and avoid under or overcooked meat.

2½ lb. pork loin
1 large onion, chopped
5 cloves garlic, minced
Hot chili peppers, minced (optional)
Salt
1 can of dark beer

Choose a roasting pan big enough to amply accommodate the roast and grease with margarine. Line it with foil and grease the foil. Rub the roast all over with the onion, garlic, peppers, and salt. Move it to the prepared pan and pile any excess onion mixture over the top. Marinate for at least 1 hour or longer.

Heat the oven to 350 degrees and put a small pan of water on the top rack in order to humidify the oven. Pour the beer over the roast and cover with aluminum foil that has two or three holes punched in for air circulation. Roast for 1 hour, or until nearly done. Remove the foil and allow the top to brown. Slice the roast, arrange on a platter, and serve with the liquid from the roasting pan, thickened if you prefer, with cornstarch. Accompany with Papaya Pepper Relish (see index).

Serves 6.

Costela de Porco com Quiabo
Pork Ribs with Okra

Okra, originating in Africa, is much loved in Brazil and appears in shrimp, chicken, and pork dishes as well as vegetable stews or simply on its own. When buying this vegetable, look for small okra about the size of a little finger and avoid very large or woody pieces.

1½ lb. country-style spareribs
4 cloves garlic, minced
½ cup vinegar
1 cup water or beef stock
1 tbsp. vegetable oil, more if necessary
1 lb. okra
Salt and pepper, to taste
½ cup water
½ cup parsley, chopped

Combine the ribs, garlic, ¼ cup vinegar, and water in a pan. Bring to a boil, cover, and cook until the meat is tender, about 1 hour. Add more water if necessary. Remove the lid from the pan and evaporate any remaining liquid, add the oil, and brown the ribs on all sides. Remove from the pan.

Top and tail the okra, then cut in small slices. Turn them into the pan in which the meat cooked and sauté briefly, then add remaining vinegar, cover, and cook for 5 minutes. Return the ribs to the pan, adjust the salt and pepper, add ½ cup of water, cover, and cook for 15 minutes to blend the flavors. Sprinkle with parsley.

Serves 3.

Lombinho de Porco com Frutas Frescas
Pork Tenderloin with Fresh Fruit

Because tenderloin is the choicest—and most expensive—cut of pork and plums are imported from Chile, this sophisticated, but easy dish, is usually reserved for guests.

1½ lb. pork tenderloin
Fresh rosemary
Fresh thyme
Salt and pepper
Olive oil
6 fresh figs
6 red plums
2 tbsp. butter
½ cup sugar
1½ cups water

With a sharp knife, slit the roast lengthwise nearly in half, insert a few branches of rosemary and thyme, close the roast, and rub the exterior with

rosemary, thyme, salt, and pepper. Brown quickly in olive oil and roast at 350 degrees for 1 hour 30 minutes or until done.

Meanwhile, cut both the figs and plums in cubes and, in separate pans, cook them each in 1 tbsp. butter, ¼ cup sugar, and ¾ cup water until the liquid has cooked down to a thick syrup.

To serve, slice the tenderloin and arrange down the center of a platter. Carefully mix the figs and plums and spoon the compote onto the meat. Serve with rice or mashed potatoes and a green vegetable.

Serves 4.

Lombo de Porco Recheado e Assado
Stuffed and Roasted Pork Loin

In the past, the four-pound pork loin, along with a whole filet mignon, always appeared on the menu at elegant dinners and big parties. In the last twenty years or so, menus have expanded and prices have risen, and as a result, large roasts are seen less frequently. This recipe is old, good, and reasonably easy to make.

Stuffing
6 strips bacon, cubed
3 tbsp. chopped onion
Salt and pepper, to taste
1 tbsp. dried sage
1 tbsp. parsley
4 cups dry breadcrumbs
½ cup chicken broth

Pork
2 lb. pork loin
4 strips bacon

Stuffing
Fry bacon and add the chopped onion and seasonings. Moisten the breadcrumbs with broth, mix with bacon mixture, and toss gently.
Pork
Split pork tenderloin in two and season with salt and pepper. Cover the bottom layer of meat with the prepared stuffing, then top with other layer of pork. Tie the

roast firmly and place 4 slices of bacon over top. Place on rack in open roasting pan, and roast in 350-degree oven for 1½ hours or until a thermometer tests done.

Serves 6.

Fígado Brasileiro
Brazilian-Style Liver

For this recipe, you need to have equal-size chunks of pineapple and peppers and the same amount of both. The best way to do this is to cut 2 or 3 ½-inch slices of pineapple, remove the core and the rind, and cut the slices into ½-inch pieces. No need to be exact: a bit more or less is fine but you want bite-size portions. Choose at least two kinds of bell peppers—red, green, yellow, or orange—preferably three or you can use all four. Slice into ½-inch pieces and dice into squares equal to the pineapple. The oil and vinegar can be the very basic oil/vinegar/salt/pepper vinaigrette you plan to use on the salad; the amount added here is very small but necessary for flavor development.

1 lb. liver
2 tbsp. vegetable oil
2 cups fresh pineapple chunks
2 cups bell pepper chunks
¼ cup water
¼ cup oil and vinegar dressing

Buy thin slices of liver, free of connecting tissue, and cut them in strips about 2 inches by ¾ inch. Sauté briefly on both sides in 1 tbsp. of oil. Remove from the skillet. Add another spoonful of oil, the pineapple, bell pepper, and water and cook over medium heat until the peppers begin to soften. Add the vinaigrette, return the liver to the pan, and reheat to a simmer. Serve immediately.

Serves 4.

Língua Gaucha
Gaucha Tongue

Emigrants from Germany and Italy settled in the state of Rio Grande do Sul, where the Italians gravitated to the Bento Gonçalves area and began to plant and cultivate vineyards. As a result, Brazil has some very acceptable wine, which has been incorporated into Brazilian cuisine for some time. When cooking with wine, choose a good one since the flavor will permeate the finished dish and determine its success. In Brazil, tongue is often sold already skinned, which allows flavors to penetrate during cooking. It is much more difficult to do this at home, but try it if you are curious about a more pronounced taste to the finished product.

3 cloves garlic, minced
1 red onion, chopped
3 tbsp. margarine
2 tbsp. tomato paste
1½ cups dry red wine
1 beef tongue, trimmed of fat and gristle
2 cups or more beef stock
Salt and pepper

In a heavy pot just big enough for the tongue, sauté the garlic and onion in margarine until translucent. Add the tomato paste and stir to incorporate. Add the wine and reduce the mixture until about ½ cup is left. Place the tongue in the pan, add enough stock to reach halfway up the meat, and cook covered until soft, around 3 hours, adding more stock if necessary. When done, taste for salt and pepper, remove the tongue, and skin it, making sure that no fat or bone remains.

Serve with the cooking liquid as a sauce; if there is too much sauce, either reduce it or thicken with a small amount of cornstarch. Mashed potatoes or banana purée are good with this dish.

Serves 6-8.

Frigideira de Mamão Verde com Carne
Sautéed Green Papaya and Meat

This is another easy main dish. According to how spicy you like your food, add more or less hot chili peppers; the dish will still be excellent.

1½ lb. ground beef
Vegetable oil as needed
2 medium onions, chopped

3 cloves garlic, minced
2 hot chili peppers, minced
1 large green pepper, chopped
2 large tomatoes, chopped
1 tbsp. vinegar
Salt and pepper
1 large, uniformly green papaya (about 2 lb.), peeled, seeded, and cut in small cubes
2 hard-boiled eggs, chopped

Sauté the meat until beginning to brown, then add the onions, garlic, and chili peppers. Sauté until the meat takes on more color and the onions are transparent; add the green pepper and tomatoes. Cook for about 10 minutes or until the tomatoes lose their rawness and the peppers begin to soften. Add the vinegar, salt, pepper, and papaya. Cook, stirring until the papaya is tender crisp. Turn into a serving bowl and sprinkle with chopped eggs. Serve with white rice.

Serves 8.

9

Desserts

Brazilian desserts range from simple to sophisticated, and many of them fail to fit easily into any category. This section presents some recipes that I feel are outstanding and would otherwise fall through the cracks. To an American, one of the most charming things about Brazilian desserts are some of the names: Mousse de Coco com Baba de Moça (Coconut Mousse with Baby's Drool); Cuca de Banana (Banana-Head); Papo de Anjo (Angel's Double-Chin); Fios de Ovo (Egg Threads); Pé de Moleque (Street-Urchin's Foot); Olho de Sogra (Mother-in-Law's Eye); Suspiro (Sigh)—these are just a few samples from a very long list.

Bolo de Sorvete de São João
São João Ice Cream Cake

A first cousin to peanut brittle, *pé do moleque* (street-urchin's foot) is popular in Brazil and is widely available in the month of June when Festa Juninas, country-western celebrations complete with costumes, games, food, and country music, are held. *Doce de leite* is condensed milk cooked until it turns a toasty brown color and is beloved by Brazilians. Of course, the simplest way to obtain this product is to buy a can, but it is not always available. In such a case, cooks in the past and in some rural areas even today emptied fresh milk and sugar into a saucepan and stirred it for two or more hours or until the desired color and taste was reached.

  1⅔ cups graham cracker crumbs
  ⅓ cup melted butter
  2 tsp. water
  2 qt. vanilla ice cream
  ⅔ cup crushed peanut brittle (can add more)
  ⅔ cup caramel milk paste (*doce de leite*) (can add more)

In a bowl, combine crumbs, butter, and water. Press firmly on bottom of an 8-inch spring-form pan or other pan or mold of your choice. Soften the ice cream and spread half in the crumb-lined pan, cover with crushed peanut brittle and *doce de leite*, then top with the remaining ice cream. Scatter more crushed peanut brittle on top and freeze.

Serves 8.

Bolo de Geléia de Berinjela
Cake with Eggplant Jelly

The original recipe for this dish was twice the size and had no directions for the jelly other than to boil the ingredients. The measurements for the dry ingredients were given in cups and liquid ingredients were given in "drinking glasses," which are not standard measurements in either country, and no mention was made of the pan size. I was intrigued by the eggplant but didn't have high hopes when I tested it. Happily, it proved to be a delightful spice cake that is a wonderful foil for ice cream or fruit and is even better when served with whipped cream. Everyone who has sampled this dessert has been enthralled; a neighbor even asked if he could put it on the menu of his bistro in the Praça Roosevelt theater district.

Jelly
1 small eggplant (about ½ lb.)
1 cup sugar
2½ cups water
1 stick cinnamon (about 2 inches long)
2 cloves
½-inch piece of ginger, peeled
1-inch piece of lemon or lime rind

Cake
1¾ cups flour
½ cup sugar
1 cup brown sugar
1 tsp. baking soda
½ tsp. cinnamon
½ tsp. nutmeg

½ tsp. grated lemon or lime rind
½ cup plus 2 tbsp. vegetable oil
¼ cup plus 2 tbsp. water
2 large eggs
½ cup eggplant jelly
1 cup dried fruit and/or nuts of your choice (raisins, apricots, dates, etc., or combination)
Powdered sugar for dusting

Jelly
Combine all the ingredients in a pan, bring to a boil, and cook over a low fire, stirring from time to time until the liquid is like syrup. Strain and reserve. (This process takes about 1 hour or so.)

Cake
Mix all the dry ingredients together in one bowl. In another, mix the oil, water,

eggs, and eggplant jelly and beat well, then combine with the dry ingredients. Stir briskly until smooth and add the dried fruit and nuts. Butter and flour a 9-inch spring-form pan with a hole in the middle and pour in the cake. Bake at 350 degrees for 1 hour or until it tests done. Allow to rest in the pan for 10 minutes and then turn out on a wire rack to cool. When cool, sift powdered sugar over the top.

Serves 10-12.

Bolo de Mel
Honey Cake

Shortly after I acquired this recipe from our friend Maya, she moved to Belo Horizonte and we lost track of one another. The memories of community work and shared meals remain, however, and are especially vivid when I bake this honey cake. Easy to make, it's much lighter than the more familiar version.

2 large eggs, or 6 small eggs
½ cup honey
½ cup (scant) vegetable oil
¼ cup plus 2 tbsp. coffee, cooled
¼ unsweetened cocoa powder
½ cup sugar
½ cup apple, peeled and grated
1 cup flour
1½ tsp. baking powder
1 ½ tsp. baking soda
1 tbsp. fruit jelly (any kind)
½ cup raisins, either light or dark
½ cup walnuts, pecans, or Brazil nuts, chopped

Separate the eggs and beat the whites stiff. In another bowl, combine all the other ingredients, including egg yolks, adding the raisins and nuts last. Fold in the beaten egg whites, turn into a greased and floured 13x9-inch baking pan, and bake at 350 degrees for 40-50 minutes or until it tests done. Cool in the pan. Serve with whipped cream if desired.

Makes 12-15 generous servings.

Bolo com Recheio de Batata-doce
Cake with Sweet Potato Filling

The first time I baked this cake I bought sweet potatoes and discovered that the flesh was purple. I had no idea that such a vegetable existed, but since then, I've been very careful to pick only the orange-fleshed yams. Although there are several steps involved in making this surprisingly light cake, it is neither difficult nor time consuming. To preserve the color of the sweet potatoes, choose light brown sugar and white rum.

Cake
¾ cup butter or margarine
1 cup sugar
3 eggs
1½ cups flour
2 tsp. baking powder
¼ cup plus 2 tbsp. milk

Filling
2 tbsp. rum
¼ cup light brown sugar
2 cups yams, cooked and mashed
2 tsp. vanilla extract
¼ cup plus 2 tbsp. butter, at room temperature

Chocolate Glaze
½ cup sugar
¼ cup corn syrup
¼ cup rum
5 oz. bittersweet chocolate, chopped

Cake
For the cake, combine the butter or margarine and sugar in a large bowl and beat with an electric beater for 5 minutes at medium speed to obtain a smooth cream. Add the eggs and beat for 3 more minutes. Mix the flour and baking powder and add to the batter, very gradually, alternating with the milk. Butter an 8-inch round baking pan with 3-inch high sides, cut wax paper to fit the bottom of the pan, and grease it

too. Pour in the batter, smooth the top, and bake at 350 degrees for 55 minutes to 1 hour or until it tests done. Cool in the pan for 10 minutes and carefully turn out onto a rack to cool. Peel the paper off the bottom and turn it right side up.

Filling

Combine all the filling ingredients and beat with an electric beater for 3 minutes to obtain a homogeneous mass. Cut the cooled cake horizontally into three equal layers. Put the bottom layer on a cake plate and top with half the filling. The easiest way to do this without tearing the cake is to drop large spoonfuls all over the cake surface and then gently connect and spread with a spatula. Add the middle layer and repeat with the remainder of the filling, then add the top layer.

Glaze

Combine the sugar, corn syrup, and rum in a small saucepan and bring to a boil. Take it off the fire, add the chocolate, and mix quickly to melt. Leave for 1-2 minutes and pour over the top of the cake, spreading quickly if necessary and allowing it to run down the sides.

Serves 12.

Bolo Fofo de Iogurte e Laranja
Soft Yogurt and Orange Cake

Vanda Pereira de Souza is a wife, mother of three small children, works in the marketing department of a São Paulo publisher, and still has the energy,

time, and talent to provide her family and friends with culinary creations. This cake is one of her many successful inventions.

Cake
4 large eggs
2 cups of sugar
½ cup margarine or butter, softened
1 ¼ cups plain yogurt
½ cup orange juice
1 tbsp. finely grated orange rind
1 tsp. vanilla extract
3 cups flour
½ tsp. salt
1 tbsp. baking powder

Glaze
1 cup confectioner's sugar
3 tbsp. orange juice
1 tbsp. lemon juice

Cake
Separate the eggs and beat the yolks, sugar, and margarine until you have a creamy, smooth mixture. Combine the yogurt, orange juice, grated orange rind, and vanilla extract. Combine the dry ingredients and add to the yolk mixture alternately with the yogurt mixture. Beat the egg whites stiff and fold delicately into the batter. Choose either an angel cake pan measuring 10

inches across the top or a spring-form pan measuring 9-10 inches with high sides and a hole in the middle; it is easier to remove the baked cake from the spring-form pan. Butter the pan well, pour in the batter, and bake at 350 degrees for about 1 hour 15 minutes or until it tests done and is golden. Remove from the pan and cool on a rack.

Glaze

Combine all the ingredients and beat smooth. After the cake has cooled to slightly warm, drizzle with the glaze, allowing it to run down the sides.

Serves 12-15.

Bolo Integral de Maçã
Whole-Wheat Apple Cake

This coffee cake is perfect for brunch or as a snack and reflects the increasing Brazilian interest in healthy foods.

2 eggs
¾ cup brown sugar
1 ½ cups whole-wheat flour (as finely ground as possible)
1 ½ tsp. cinnamon
1½ tsp. baking powder
½ tsp. salt
2 apples, peeled, cored, and finely chopped
¾ cup light raisins
6 tbsp. vegetable oil

With an electric beater on high, beat the eggs for 5 minutes until they are thick and light colored. Little by little, add the sugar, continuing to beat.

Mix the flour, cinnamon, baking powder, and salt and then add the apples and raisins. Add this mixture to the eggs, alternately with the oil. Pour the batter into a greased and floured round, 8-inch baking pan with high sides and bake at 350 degrees for 50 minutes to 1 hour or until it tests done.

Remove from the pan when it is cold.

Serves 8-10.

Torta de Ricotta
Ricotta Pie

This recipe was given to me by my good friend, the artist Jean Smith, who lived and worked in São Paulo for more than fifty years. She had ricotta delivered directly to her from a small dairy farm that specialized in making cheese. One day when he brought her order, the farmer gave Jean this recipe, a long-time favorite of his family.

1 lb. fresh ricotta
1 can sweetened condensed milk
3 tbsp. cornstarch
Grated lemon peel
4 eggs, separated

Beat everything, except the egg whites, in the blender until smooth. Beat the egg whites stiff and fold into the ricotta mixture. Pour into a round, 10-inch form (not a pie plate) that has been greased and floured. Bake at 325 degrees for approximately 1 hour. Cool and chill well before serving.

Serves 8.

Doce de Leite Sorvete
Caramel Ice Cream

Paulistanos adore both ice cream and *doce de leite;* the crunchy bits in this dessert are an added bonus. *Doce de leite* may be purchased at a store selling Latino food products or through the sources guide.

1 cup sugar
1 cup nuts, either cashew or Brazil, chopped
1 can (10 oz.) *doce de leite*
1⅓ cups milk
1¼ cups heavy cream
½ tsp. vanilla extract

In a saucepan, melt the sugar over very low heat, stirring constantly. Add the chopped nuts and cook for several more minutes, still over very low heat, until the color is caramel brown. Immediately remove from the fire, pour it onto a well-greased granite or marble surface, and allow to cool. When completely cold, break it up using either a rolling pin or a rubber kitchen hammer or both. The pieces should be quite small.

When the nut mixture is cold, beat the *doce de leite,* milk, cream, and vanilla extract together, then process in an ice cream machine. Mix in the sugar/nut mixture and freeze.

Serves 6-8.

Torta Paulista
Paulista Pie

Pavés are wonderful layered desserts, usually made from cookies with creams and/or fruit. This one is typical of those made throughout Brazil and is a good one for groups as it can be made a day ahead and easily doubled.

½ cup butter
1 cup sugar
2 large egg yolks
1 cup sour cream
8 oz. ladyfinger cookies or Champagne biscuits
1 can (10 oz.) *doce de leite* (caramelized milk paste)

Mix first 3 ingredients. Add sour cream and mix well. In an 8-inch, square casserole place 1 layer of cookies, a layer of cream mixture, another layer of cookies, and the rest of the mixture. Add another layer of cookies and cover all with the *doce de leite.* Refrigerate overnight.

Serves 8.

Pudim de Canela com Molho de Frutas
Cinnamon Pudding with Fruit Sauce

There are several varieties of tangerines in Brazil, and they are usually peeled and eaten as a snack or used in juice. This unusual sauce is also delicious over vanilla or any fruit ice cream and can also be used to enhance rice pudding or baked custard. This freezes beautifully.

Sauce
14 oz. carrots
1 cup water
½ cup sugar
1-2 passion fruit
2½ cups fresh tangerine juice

Pudding
1½ cups milk
1 tsp. cinnamon
1 stick cinnamon
1 can sweetened condensed milk
4 eggs

Sauce

Cook the carrots with the water and sugar. Cool in their liquid. To obtain about ⅔ cup passion fruit juice (or according to taste), scrape out the pulp and whirl it in the blender, then strain to remove the seeds. Put the carrots, their cooking liquid, tangerine juice, and passion fruit juice in the blender and blend until smooth. Chill.

Pudding

Bring the milk, the powdered cinnamon, and stick cinnamon to a boil, then turn off the fire and discard the stick. When the milk has cooled to warm, beat the condensed milk and eggs together and gradually add the cinnamon milk. If necessary to incorporate the powdered cinnamon completely, whirl in the blender. Pour into 8 small ceramic ramekins, greased and coated with sugar, and bake in a hot water bath at 350 degrees for 30-45 minutes or until a table knife inserted in the center comes out almost clean. Remove from the oven, transfer to a cold water bath to stop the cooking, and chill. To serve, unmold on individual plates and surround with plenty of sauce.

Serves 8.

Morango com Chantilly
Strawberries with Whipped Cream

This is another traditional dish with many variations, some of which are quite elaborate. This one is simple but impressive, with just three layered components. Although the recipe for no-fail meringues is given here, you could also use purchased meringues. This is an extremely flexible dessert recipe, and amounts of all ingredients can be increased or decreased as needed or according to taste.

2 large egg whites*
4 tbsp. sugar
10 oz. fresh strawberries
1 cup heavy cream

Beat the egg whites really stiff. Beat in half the sugar and beat again. Fold in the remaining sugar. Cover the baking pan with parchment paper and drop the egg whites in 3-inch rounds. Bake at 240 degrees for 1½ hours. Cool.

Cut large strawberries in quarters and smaller ones in half. Just before serving, whip the cream and layer the meringues, strawberries, and whipped cream on individual serving plates in the following order:

1. Meringue
2. Whipped Cream
3. Strawberries
4. Whipped cream
5. Meringue
6. Whipped cream
7. Strawberries

If you prefer, the meringues may be broken into pieces or even crumbled before layering. Serve immediately or the meringue will absorb moisture and melt.

If you are storing egg whites, ⅓ cup equals 2 large whites.

Servings are variable and depend on the amount made. The 2-egg meringue given above will serve 4-6 people.

10

Miscellaneous

There are many bits and pieces of Brazilian cuisine that can't be incorporated into a category but are very important as part of the culture. This cookbook would be incomplete without recipes for some of the sauces, children's candies, drinks, and other foods that play an essential role in the lives of these South American people. Although it is unnecessary to include a recipe for coffee, anyone interested in the food of Brazil should be advised that a *cafezinho*, or little coffee, is mandatory after lunch and dinner and is offered to visitors as a courteous welcome. Always freshly made, it is often drunk midmorning and/or in the afternoon. This coffee is very strong, very sweet, and always served in demitasse cups. Since the drink is so strong, refills are unknown. Unable to brew their coffee just prior to drinking it, feira workers arrive with the hot beverage in a thermos and fortify themselves from time to time with coffee in tiny paper cups. And it is made from homegrown coffee beans from the state of São Paulo that are roasted, finely ground, packaged, and available in every market.

Molho Brasileiro
Brazilian Sauce

This sauce is served, literally, with everything—chicken, roasts, seafood, salads, and vegetables. To Brazilians, this sauce is almost as indispensable as the saltshaker and, in restaurants, often appears on the table together with salt, oil, and vinegar. I like this sauce on roasts or grilled fish and a few spoonfuls will enliven an oil-and-vinegar salad dressing.

Juice of 3 limes
½ red bell pepper, minced
½ medium onion, minced
¼ cup parsley, minced
Salt, to taste
¼ cup fresh cilantro, minced
1 tomato, peeled, seeded, and chopped
2 green onions, minced
Hot pepper, minced, to taste, or hot pepper sauce
3 tbsp. olive oil

Mix and allow to rest for at least 1 hour to blend the flavors.
Makes 1½-2 cups.

Caldo do Frango
Chicken Stock

This can be made either with chicken bones, including the back, feet, and neck if available, or with a whole chicken. A friendly butcher will often provide the bones, but if you prefer to experiment with an entire chicken, choose an old stewing hen that requires long simmering to tenderize rather than a young bird that will toughen and lose all flavor in this particular cooking process. When freezing the broth, it's a good idea to use an ice cube tray for at least some of the stock so that small amounts can be quickly thawed for use in sauces. After the cubes are frozen, transfer them to a plastic bag, seal tightly, and use as necessary.

1 medium chicken, or 1-1½ lb. bones
1 onion, sliced
1 carrot, sliced
1 tomato, chopped
4 parsley sprigs
2 tsp. salt
1 tbsp. black peppercorns
4 qt. water
1 tbsp. vinegar

Wash the chicken or bones and combine with all the other ingredients in a large pot. There should be enough water to cover by 3 inches. Bring to a boil, skim off the foam, lower the heat, partially cover the pot, and cook for 2-2½ hours. Cool, strain, and chill. Skim the fat from the surface and either use within 4 days or freeze.

Makes about 3 qt.

Churrasco Vinagrette
Sauce for Grilled Steak

Churrascos, or barbecues, are a Brazilian institution, and as in other South American countries, the chef is traditionally male. No barbecue is complete without lots of this sauce accompanying the meat along with *farofa* (for *farofa* recipes, see index).

2 cups onion, finely chopped
1 clove garlic, impaled on a toothpick
¾ cup olive oil
½ cup or less red wine
3 tbsp. chopped parsley
1 tbsp. chopped cilantro
Salt, to taste
1 cup chopped tomato

Mix all ingredients, except tomatoes, and let stand. Just before serving, add tomatoes and take out the garlic clove. For a lighter sauce, replace some of the wine with water.

Makes about 3 cups.

Palmito e Azeitonas Verdes
Palmito and Green Olives

This is an accompaniment for cocktails. If you keep a can or jar of *palmito* and some olives on hand, you will never have to wonder what to serve to unexpected guests. Rosa, our feira vendor for fresh herbs, advised removing the leaves from basil, packing them loosely into plastic containers, and storing in the freezer. When you pluck the frozen leaves, they are not exactly like fresh but very close and always available.

Palmito, sliced on the diagonal in ½- to ¾-inch slices
Whole green olives, without pits
Fresh basil leaves
Olive oil

Arrange the palmito and olives on an attractive serving plate, scatter with basil leaves, and pour a good amount of olive oil over all. Have toothpicks and either Italian bread or crackers available.

Miscellaneous

Beijinhos de Coco
Little Coconut Kisses

Birthday parties in Brazil, especially for children, are as important, or more so, than Christmas. It's a part of the culture, and those invited to parties include not just friends of the celebrant, but the entire family of each guest. Parties are frequently enormous and those for children are replete with sweets and more sweets. Adeline Remy, a distinguished cook, made these Little Coconut Kisses so many times while her two sons were growing up that the recipe is indelibly imprinted in her memory.

2 tbsp. unsalted butter
1 can sweetened condensed milk
¼ cup unsweetened grated coconut
Additional coconut for coating
Whole cloves

In a saucepan, melt the butter. Add the condensed milk, cook, and stir constantly with a wooden spoon until the mixture is thick and leaves the bottom of the pan. Remove from the heat and add ¼ cup coconut. Cool.

Sprinkle additional coconut over the surface of a plate. With a teaspoon, scoop up small portions of the coconut mixture and, with well-buttered hands, form them into balls. Roll in coconut and then either place each Little Kiss in a tiny paper cup or arrange them on a platter. Traditionally, a single clove is placed on top of each.

Makes about 30.

Brigadeiros
Brigadeiros

The mere thought of a *brigadeiro* will bring a sparkle to the eyes and a smile to the lips of Brazilians to whom this sweet is a comfort food from earliest memories. Mandatory at children's birthday parties, these also appear at adult events of all kinds and, of course, at home.

1 can sweetened condensed milk
4 tbsp. powdered unsweetened cocoa
1 tbsp. butter
Crystallized sugar or chocolate sprinkles

Mix the ingredients thoroughly over a medium fire, stirring constantly with a wooden spoon. When the bottom of the pan appears with each scrape of the spoon, turn off the fire. With oiled hands, roll the mass into small balls. Roll the balls in crystallized sugar or chocolate sprinkles.

Makes about 35.

Gourmet Farofa de Caju
Farofa with Bread and Cashews

Although traditional *farofa* consists simply of toasted manioc meal, there are countless versions of this essential condiment that can be sprinkled over just about everything. This is one of the more unusual, tasty, and sophisticated *farofas* and is served at a barbecue alongside the meat where it soaks up some of the juices.

4 cups cubed Italian bread
12 basil leaves
Salt, to taste
3 tbsp. olive oil
4 oz. cashews, roasted

Preheat oven to 400 degrees and place the bread cubes in a roasting pan. Toss with basil leaves, salt, and olive oil. Toast bread cubes in the oven for about 20 minutes or until lightly browned. When cubes are slightly cool, put in a processor with cashews and process until mixture becomes coarse breadcrumbs.

Makes about 3 cups.

Caipirinha
Caipirinha

This is the national drink and is made with lime, sugar, sugar cane *cachaça*, and ice. Because the drink is individually mixed, unlike sangrias that are made and served in a pitcher, each person can vary the ingredients according to their taste. It is not uncommon to substitute vodka for *cachaça*, and in this case, the drink becomes a *caipiroshka*. Derivan Ferreira de Souza is one of the most respected bartenders in Brazil. Two-time president of the Brazilian Barmen's Association, he

represented the International Bartenders Association in Latin America for six years and has standardized the *caipirinha* as follows.

1 medium lime, cut into small cubes without the core
2 tbsp. bar sugar
1½ oz. *cachaça*
Ice cubes or crushed ice

Place the lime pieces and sugar in the bottom of an old-fashioned glass and crush with a pestle. Add the *cachaça* and crushed ice or cubes and stir.
Serves 1.

Caipirinha Arretada
Spicy Hot *Caipirinha*

This is a very sophisticated version of the classic *Caipirinha*, found only in the major cities of Brazil.

2 strawberries, sliced
½ kiwi, sliced
Sugar, to taste
1 small hot red pepper
1½ oz. *cachaça*

Put the sliced fruits in the glass, saving one slice of kiwi to decorate the edge of the glass. Gently mash the fruits together with the sugar. Add the seeded red pepper and the *cachaça*. Mix well and fill glass with ice.
Serves 1.

Manga-Melão Samba
Mango-Melon Samba

Juice bars are found all over São Paulo, and all the drinks served are made from fresh fruit. The combinations are limited only by the imagination, but here is one of the most requested.

Mango, any kind
Melon, any kind
Hot chili pepper

In a blender, add equal quantities of mango and melon flesh and add a relatively small piece of a hot chili pepper. Blend until smooth; the flavor should be exotic rather than noticeably spicy.

Serves 1.

Abacaxi com Hortelã
Pineapple and Mint Cooler

Here is another juice bar classic that is very refreshing on a hot day.

Fresh pineapple juice
Mint leaves
Sprig of mint

Whirl the juice and leaves in a blender and garnish with a sprig of mint.

Serves 1.

Empadas de Palmito
Hearts of Palm Empanadas

These are often small and served as hors d'oeuvres with cocktails or at parties. Although, accompanied by a salad, larger empanadas make a very satisfying light lunch.

Dough
1 cup flour
1 tsp. baking powder
¼ tsp. salt
¼ cup butter

Filling
2 cups hearts of palm, finely chopped
½ medium onion, finely chopped
1 clove garlic, minced
2 medium tomatoes, peeled, seeded, and finely chopped
2 tbsp. finely chopped parsley
¼ cup olives, minced
½ tsp. salt

Dough

Preheat oven to 375 degrees. Sift all dry ingredients together and add the butter, either cutting it in with a pastry cutter or crumbling with the fingers. Roll out the dough and cut into circles. Cut the dough into very small circles for hor d'oeuvres, or into about 6-inch circles for a lunch or snack.

Filling

Chop the hearts of palm finely. Lightly sauté the onion and garlic and, when transparent, add the tomatoes, parsley, and olives. Sauté for a few more minutes and add the hearts of palm and salt. Cook for another few minutes and cool. Place some of the cooled filling on the dough and fold over, first wetting the edges of the circle to firmly seal.

Bake turnovers in the oven for 30 minutes or until the tops are lightly browned.

Makes 5 6-inch empanadas.

Torta de Ricota e Presunto
Ricotta and Ham Pie

With a toasted breadcrumb crust, this ham and cheese pie is perfect for a light lunch. In Brazil, ham is sold in paper-thin slices and is torn by hand into bits for this dish, a process that can be approximated by either shredding or finely chopping the ham.

Crust
3 cups whole-wheat breadcrumbs, oven-toasted and cooled
⅓ cup grated Parmesan cheese
Salt
⅓ cup butter or margarine

Filling
2 red onions, finely chopped
2 tbsp. oil
1 cup cooked baked ham, shredded or finely chopped
1 lb. ricotta
⅔ cup yogurt
½ cup flour
3 eggs, beaten
⅓ cup grated Parmesan cheese
10 basil leaves, chopped

Crust

Mix the breadcrumbs and Parmesan. Add a pinch of salt and the melted butter. Mix well and pat onto the sides and bottom of a round, 10-inch cake or pie dish and press to compact.

Filling

Sauté the onions in oil until transparent, add the ham, and sauté very briefly. Cool. Meanwhile, combine the ricotta, yogurt, flour, and eggs and beat smooth. Add the Parmesan, basil, and the ham/onion mixture. Taste for salt, mix thoroughly, and spread over the crumb crust. Bake at 350 degrees for 1 hour or until the filling is firm. Allow it to cool to room temperature and serve with a green salad.

Serves 8.

Pão de Claudia
Claudia's Bread

A few years ago, my husband and I spent a long weekend at a lovely *pousada* (bed and breakfast), or inn, in São Pedro do Aldeia, a village on a large salt lake close to the sea about a hundred miles north of Rio de Janeiro. Our room overlooked the lake, where we swam and paddled kayaks, and we napped in hammocks on our terrace. This fabulous bread was among the array of delicious breakfast dishes created and provided by Claudia, the cook at that time. Thanks to her generosity in sharing the recipe, we have been able to duplicate the bread many times, although never for breakfast. A delightful dish for a spring or summer lunch, this must always be served warm and is best with a cold soup to start and a salad to accompany it.

1 tbsp. yeast
½ cup warm water
1 egg
1 tsp. salt
1 tbsp. vegetable oil
1¾ cups (½ lb.) flour
1 cup tomatoes, peeled, seeded, and chopped
1½-2 cups mozzarella, chopped
2 tbsp. chopped fresh basil leaves

Dissolve the yeast in water. Add the egg and salt and mix well. Then add the oil and flour. Knead for about 5 minutes on a well-floured board, adding more flour if necessary. Roll dough into a ball and let rise in a greased bowl for about 45 minutes. When double in bulk, punch the dough down and roll it into a rectangle approximately 8 inches by 14 inches. Pat the tomatoes and cheese as dry as possible with paper towels, then distribute on the surface of the dough, sprinkling with basil. Roll up and seal by moistening the edges and pinching together. Let it rise again for about 30 minutes and bake at 350 degrees for 25-30 minutes.

Serves 6.

Pão de Queijo
Brazilian Cheese Bread

These popular rolls can be found all over the states of Rio, Minas Gerais, and São Paulo and are made with Parmesan, mozzarella, or Minas Gerais cheese. This recipe uses *polvilho doce* flour (see sources),

which is actually a starch from the manioc root. Unlike the flours we are accustomed to using, this has an odd, silky texture and is best mixed by the hand rather than a spoon.

1½ cups milk
⅓ cup vegetable oil
3½ cups *polvilho doce* flour, approximately
1 tsp. salt
2 eggs
8 oz. mozzarella cheese, grated
2 oz. Parmesan cheese, grated

Bring the milk and oil to a boil, turn off the fire, and gradually add the flour and salt, stirring with a wooden spoon. It will be lumpy and sticky. When it is cool enough, mix and squeeze by hand. Add the eggs, one at a time, still mixing and squeezing by hand, and then the cheese and more flour. When you have a cohesive mass, knead briefly. It will still be lumpy but don't worry. Let it rest for 30 minutes, then form into balls, arrange on an ungreased baking sheet, and bake at 350 degrees for 25 minutes or until golden.

Makes about 32 rolls.

Molho de Papaia e Pimentão
Papaya Pepper Relish

Brazilians frequently serve roast pork, and this relish is a perfect complement to the meat.

1 papaya, peeled, seeded, and diced
1 roasted red bell pepper, diced
3 green chilies, finely chopped, or to taste
1 small red onion, diced
Juice of 1 lime
2 tsp. rice vinegar
2 tsp. honey
Salt and pepper, to taste

In a large bowl, combine all the ingredients. Just before serving, toss relish quickly in sauté pan to warm (do not overheat).

Makes 2 cups.

Pão de Minuto
Minute Bread

Brazilians like to have bread with all meals. These rolls, made with baking powder rather than yeast, are quick to make and are often found on the table for the main meal at noon or as a snack in the evening and are best eaten on the day they are baked. A Brazilian woman was once heard commenting to her friends about a new maid/cook: "She won't last long. She doesn't even know how to make *pão de minuto*!"

1¾ cups flour
2 large eggs
2 tbsp. butter or margarine
½ cup plus 2 tbsp. milk
1 tsp. salt
1 tbsp. baking powder

Preheat oven to 400 degrees. Place everything in a bowl and mix all with a beater or processor. Fill well-greased muffin cups ¾ full and bake for about 25 minutes.

Note: These rolls adapt well to one or two of the following additions: 1 tbsp. each of oregano, finely sliced green onion, Parmesan cheese, or chopped olives. For sweet bread, add diced dried fruits with a little sugar.

Makes about 10.

Tempero Brasileiro
Brazilian Spice

Every feira has one or two mini-stands where an infinite variety of dried spices in covered plastic containers are sold. The proprietor grinds peppercorns to order, mixes spices on demand, and offers homemade, paralyzingly spicy chili sauce for sale. Brazilian Spice is so popular that Anailde, owner of

this particular stand, has a ready-mixed container on display but willingly gave me the recipe when I explained that North Americans had no way to purchase this seasoning agent. Keep this in a small jar with a tight lid in a dark, cool place, and it will retain its flavor for weeks.

Oregano
Parsley
Coriander
Basil
Marjoram
Red pepper flakes

Combine equal amounts of the dried spices. Finely grind in a spice or coffee grinder until powdery. Brazilians like this to be very spicy, so taste it and feel free to add more red pepper flakes if you like.

Cuscuz Paulista
São Paulo Couscous

There are many versions of this very Brazilian dish ranging from sweet to savory, and none of them bears much resemblance to the original North African couscous, which was brought to Brazil by the Portuguese. In fact, it doesn't even use actual couscous, which is termed, in Brazil, *cuzcuz marroquinho* or Moroccan couscous. This is a molded pudding and a popular first course in São Paulo.

1 lb. medium shrimp, cleaned
4 tbsp. oil
2 cups cornmeal, or ½ cup manioc flour and 1 ½ cups cornmeal
1 ½ cups fish stock (about)
1 can sardines in oil, oil reserved
2 tbsp. dried shrimp
2 tomatoes
1 onion, chopped
1 clove garlic, minced
½ cup black olives, sliced
½ cup green olives, sliced and stuffed
1 cup frozen peas

1 cup frozen corn, cooked
1 cup *palmito*, thinly sliced
2 hard-boiled eggs, sliced
1 lettuce, kale, or cabbage leaf

Sauté the shrimp in 2 tbsp. oil and reserve. In a bowl, combine the cornmeal and manioc flour (if using the latter) and, using the fingers, work in enough fish stock and some of the sardine oil to dampen. Finely grind the dried shrimp in a coffee grinder or food processor and reserve. Thinly slice 1 tomato and chop the other tomato. Sauté the onion and garlic in the remaining oil, then add the dried ground shrimp and chopped tomato. Cook for a few minutes, take off the heat, and stir in 1 tbsp. black olives and 1 tbsp. green olives, then add to the cornmeal mixture along with the peas and corn.

Oil a round colander with small holes or a steamer with small holes and decorate the bottom and lower half with the sautéed shrimp and half the sardines and slices of palmito, tomato, olives, and egg. Carefully spoon half the cornmeal mixture into the colander and press down gently. Arrange the remaining sardines, palmito, tomato, olives, and egg along the upper sides of the colander and fill with the rest of the cornmeal. Cover the top with a lettuce, kale, or cabbage leaf and seal it with an aluminum foil "lid." Place over a pot of simmering water; do not let the bottom of the colander touch the water. Put the lid on the pot and steam for 30 minutes, rest for 5 minutes, then invert on a plate and cut serving slices with a sharp knife.

Serves 6-8.

Figos Cristalizados
Crystallized Figs

This recipe was given to me by Lenina Pomeranz who gave no specific quantities for the ingredients since they can be expanded or contracted at will. This recipe is typical of Brazilian fruits and some vegetables—mainly squash—that are cooked in heavy sugar syrup.

Sugar
Water
Green figs (not black)
Crystallized sugar

Use 3 parts sugar to 1 part water and boil until it is hot enough to spin a thread. The easiest and most exact way to determine this is with a candy thermometer, which should read 230 degrees. Add the figs, lower the heat, and cook until the figs are soft, stirring occasionally. Remove and roll in crystallized sugar. Cool and serve as dessert, either alone or with a soft cheese, such as ricotta or goat cheese.

Glossary

Bacalhau

Brought from Portugal four hundred years ago, salted, air-dried codfish has been an integral part of Brazilian cuisine ever since. However, soaring prices have now lifted it into the luxury class. When buying, look for firm, white flesh, preferably in blocks, which are usually free of skin and most spines (yellow color indicates age). Salt cod must be soaked in fresh, cold water to cover for at least twelve hours, and twenty-four hours if possible. Change the water four or five times, then boil the fish in fresh, cold water for twenty minutes, drain, and shred.

Cachaça

This distilled alcohol made from sugar cane, also known as *pinga* in Brazilian slang and *aguardente* in correct Portuguese, has a distinctive flavor. In the past, it was known as the "poor man's drink"—because it cost almost nothing—and was extremely rough. Today it is quite popular, and the quality runs the gamut from fairly rough to a smooth equivalent of fine cognac, with a price range to match.

Camarão seco

In Brazil, these shrimp, dipped in *dendê* oil, are sun-dried in the state of Bahia. Small amounts are usually ground and added to dishes with an African origin where their flavor is particularly important. Occasionally, they are sold packed in salt and, in this case, need to be thoroughly rinsed before using. In the U.S. dried shrimp can be found in Asian, West Indian, and African markets.

Carne seca

Also called *charque, carne do sol,* and jerked beef, this salted meat is sun- and air-dried in a rigidly prescribed process that is totally different from the one used for American beef jerky; the two are not interchangeable. Like *bacalhau,* the dried cod described above, *carne seca* must be desalted before use, but the soaking period is just overnight with three changes of water. The meat is then cooked in fresh, cold water until tender—usually three hours. The flavor is distinctive and there is no substitute; it is obtainable in some Latino markets or through online stores.

Dendê oil

According to popular belief, the *dendê* palm was brought to Brazil by African slaves and is the only nonindigenous palm tree in the country. The oil, high in saturated fat and produced from the palm nuts, has a unique flavor when heated and is used extensively in the cuisine of Bahia. There is no substitute for this oil. However, when preparing dishes that call for *dendê* and an authentic flavor is necessary, I use either vegetable or olive oil for cooking and add just one or two teaspoons of *dendê* when the dish is nearly finished. With this tiny amount, the distinctive flavor comes through without incurring a danger of elevated cholesterol levels. Usually, I eliminate the oil altogether and find the dishes equally delicious, although probably a tad less authentic.

Doce de leite

Beloved by Brazilians, this thick, sweet syrup made from milk and sugar is used in a number of desserts. Previously prepared in the home by boiling milk and sugar until very thick and caramel colored, it became available in cans some time ago. It can be found in Latino markets or online sources.

Farofa

Basic *farofa* is manioc meal toasted in a dry skillet or lightly sautéed in butter, olive oil, or *dendê* oil and is sprinkled over chicken, rice, beans, meat, and fish. There are endless variations and additions to this simple recipe and a few include cornmeal rather than manioc meal. At buffets and in restaurants, one always sees *farofa* in one form or another, and it usually appears at mealtimes in Brazilian homes.

Mandioca

Called manioc, yuca, and cassava in North America, this tuber has been the major food staple for centuries in South America. Sold fresh in Latin American markets, it is long and thick and has a rough, dark brown skin and white flesh. To cook raw manioc, peel, cut into large chunks, and boil until tender, then carefully remove the central cord and mash or prepare according to the recipe. Manioc flour is actually a coarse meal, sold both toasted or untoasted, and is used in *farofas* and as a thickening agent in some stews, purées, and sauces.

Pimenta malagueta

Although many varieties of hot chili peppers are grown and used in Brazil, the fiery *malagueta* is arguably the hottest and most widely used. These chilies are bottled commercially and sold in all supermarkets. Fresh, they are combined with oil and vinegar and appear in small dishes in both the home and in restaurants, where drops of the liquid or the actual chilies may be added to beans, stews, and other dishes. When dealing with them, as with any chili, use rubber gloves since the oil can irritate and mildly burn the skin. If the oil should make any contact with the eyes, wash immediately with fresh, cold water.

Sources of Brazilian Food Ingredients and Products

The availability of Brazilian cooking ingredients has increased dramatically in the United States, with the increased immigration of Brazilians to cities like Miami, Boston, New York, Los Angeles, and Washington D.C. The census of 1990 counted 65,875 Brazilians living in the U.S. In 2008, the official count had increased to 351,914.

Internet Retailers (distributes throughout U.S.)

Amigo Foods
www.amigofoods.com
Miami, FL
800-627-2544

Brazil by the Bay Market
www.brazilbythebaymartket.com
sales@brazilbythebaymarket.com
3770 Hancock Street
San Diego, CA 92110
619-692-0120

Local Food Markets

New York City
Rio Bonito—Grocery Store
3215 36th Avenue
Astoria, NY 11106
718-728-4300

Coisa Nossa
47 W. 46th Street
New York, NY 10036
212-719-4779
800-745-0623

Seabra's Supermarket
www.seabrasupermarkets.com
260 Lafayette Street
Newark, NJ 07105
973-589-8606

Emporium Brasil
15 W. 46th Street
New York, NY 10036
212-764-4646

U.S. Brazil Deli & Grocery
Sunnyside
4102 34th Avenue
Long Island City, NY 11101
718-482-0219

Boston Area

International Market
366 Somerville Avenue
Somerville, MA 02143
617-776-1880

U.S.A. and Brasil Market
77 Bow Street
Somerville, MA 02134
617-776-5000

Aqui Brasil Market
139 Brighton Avenue, Suite 5
Allston, MA 02134
617-787-0758

Chicago

Supermercado Pepe's
2335 N. Western Avenue
Logan Square
Chicago, IL 60647
773-278-8756

Brasil Legal—Grocery Store
Logan Square
2153 N. Western Avenue
Chicago, IL 60647
773-772-6650

La Unica Food Market
Edgewater
1515 W Devon Avenue
Chicago, IL 60660
773-274-7788

Los Angeles

Super King Markets
www.superkingmarkets.com
Glassell Park
2716 N. San Fernando Road
Los Angeles, CA 90065
323-225-0044

Kitanda Brazil Market
Sherman Oaks
13715 Ventura Boulevard
Sherman Oaks, CA 91423
818-995-7422

San Francisco

Mercado Brasil
Mission
1252 Valencia Street
San Francisco, CA 94110
415-641-3066

22nd & Irving Market
Outer Sunset
2101 Irving Street
San Francisco, CA 94122
415-681-5212

Evergreen Super Market
Mission
2539 Mission Street
San Francisco, CA 94110
415-641-4506

Via Brazil
1770-A Lombard Street
San Francisco, CA 94123
415-673-7744

Washington D.C. Area

By Brasil
www.bybrazilmd.com
info@bybrazilmd.com
Service Area: Silver Spring, Washington, D.C., and Virginia
11333 Georgia Avenue
Silver Spring, MD 20902
866-638-3090

United Kingdom

Brazilian Products
www.brazilianproducts.co.uk
24 Friars Entry
Oxford
44-1865-243017

Super Mercado Portugal
www.supermercadoportugal.com
396 Harrow Road
Maida Vale
London
44-2072-896620

Index